EXECUTIVE JOB SEARCH IN THE HIDDEN JOB MARKET

THE MORITA METHOD

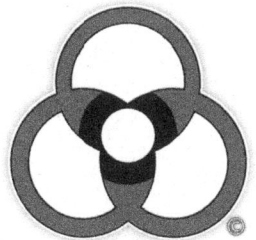

RAINER MORITA

Copyright ©2018 by Rainer Morita, All rights reserved.

All rights reserved. No part of this report may be reproduced or transmitted in any form by any means, electronically or mechanically, including photocopying, recording, retrieval system, without prior written permission from the author.

ISBN-13: 978-1515224433
ISBN-10: 1515224430

The only intent of the authors is to offer information to help you improve your life. The choices you make are entirely up to you. The author assumes no responsibility for the results of your actions.

Editor: Jacob Kose

Library of Congress Cataloging-in-Publication Data:

1. Job hunting 2. Career changes 3. Job Markets & Advice

Executive Job Search in the Hidden Job Market - The Morita Method

Authored by Rainer Morita

ISBN-13: 978-1515224433

ISBN-10: 1515224430

LCCN: 2015916460

*For
Akira Koudate*

TABLE OF CONTENTS

About the Author 7

Foreword 9

Step 1: Job Search the Hidden Job Market

    1.1 The Hidden Job Market 11

    1.2 The New Job Search Economics 17

    1.3 Outsource to Get an Edge 20

Step 2: Discover and Design Your Perfect Job

    2.1 Know What You Want 23

    2.2 Define Your Perfect Job Using the Job Temple 24

    2.3 Prioritize Your Pillars 30

Step 3: Targeting

    3.1 Identifying Industries and Locations 33

    3.2 Finding Hidden Information 40

    3.3 Direct Mail 45

    3.4 Building Your Mailing List 50

Step 4: Communicating Your Value

    4.1 Create an Irresistible Unique Value Proposition 57

    4.2 Communicating Your Unique Value Proposition 63

    4.3 Mailing Your Documents 70

Step 5: Meeting the Decision-maker

    5.1 Peak Performance Interviewing In The Hidden Job Market . . 73

    5.2 The Growth Agenda. 77

    5.3 Interview Follow-Up That Sets You Apart 86

    5.4 Finalizing the Offer. 88

    5.5 On-Board Support 90

Conclusion 93

Appendix 1: Other Job Search Channels

    Other Channel 1: Cold Calling 98

    Other Channel 2: Executive Recruiters 101

    Other Channel 3: LinkedIn 104

    Other Channel 4: Personal Contacts 106

    Other Channel 5: Networking 108

    Other Channel 6: Targeted Networking 111

Appendix 2: Sample Value Proposition Letter

    Sample China CEO Value Proposition Letter 116

    Sample Emerging Markets CEO, India Value Proposition Letter . . 117

Appendix 3: List of Questions for Research Meetings

Appendix 4: Sample Thank-You Letter

ENDNOTES 127

ABOUT THE AUTHOR

Rainer Morita

www.MoritaMethod.com

International Job Search Coach & Hidden Job Market Expert

Seminar Leader & Keynote Speaker

Professional Resume Writer

Executive Search Consultant

Rainer Morita is an International Job Search Coach and Hidden Job Market Expert who partners with top-tier executives worldwide to secure perfect jobs based on his proprietary job search approach called the Morita Method. Rainer operates his global business from the heart of Dubai.

As executive search agent, he is working for one of the largest executive search firms in search of mission-critical leadership talent. Rainer has become a gateway to Asia for European firms, and to Europe for Asian firms.

He is an International Bestseller Author who authored four books: *"Executive Job Search in the Hidden Job Market - The Morita Method"*, *"Peak Performance Interviewing for Executives"*, *"Globalization Opportunities for Executives in Japanese Companies"* and *"Find Your Career Passion."*

You can contact him at **contact@moritamethod.com.**

FOREWORD

After 15 years of executive job searching and interviewing over 5,000 executives, I have come to realize that most executives make some terrible mistakes when searching for a job. Most of them are unsuccessful in their job search because they only search for open jobs. The secret to helping them, I have concluded, is targeting invisible or hidden jobs. This is because at least 90% of all job opportunities for executives are in what is called the Hidden Job Market.

Unfortunately, there is a disconnect in the Hidden Job Market. Only top managers who are well-known or in demand get regularly approached for these hidden opportunities. The vast majority of executives seeking new jobs remain unknown to decision-makers and are therefore essentially locked out of the hiring conversation.

These people need to become proactive. But they also need the right approach. I have therefore developed and refined the Morita Method for executives to secure opportunities in the Hidden Job Market. The Morita Method maximizes your time, skills, network and professional accomplishments to get you an executive job in the Hidden Job Market within 120 days.

STEP 1:
JOB SEARCH THE HIDDEN JOB MARKET

1.1 THE HIDDEN JOB MARKET

The Hidden Job Market is THE job market for top management. Over my years as an Executive Job Search Recruiter, I have found that over 90% of manager positions (those that pay over USD $150,000) are in the Hidden Job Market. On the other hand, when have you seen CEOs positions listed in the Open Job Market (web portals, job sites, etc.)?

> **THE HIDDEN JOB MARKET HAS OVER 90% OF SENIOR MANAGER POSITIONS.**

The Hidden Job Market Versus The Open Job Market

There is a constant coming and going of hidden job opportunities not visible to the outside world. Often, such hidden opportunities exist for several months. That is the time it takes a decision-maker to actually realize the need to hire someone and the time elapsed for the organization to actually hire a person. The moment an organization discloses a job to the public, it accesses the Open Job Market. The Open Job Market includes printed media, such as classifieds, or online media, such as job boards, LinkedIn, Twitter, and corporate websites. It also includes all non-confidential searches by recruiting agencies. However, these actions are often a last resort, long after the Hidden Job Market has been exhausted.

Where Do Jobs Hide?

Hidden job opportunities arise because of an organization's need to A) fuel growth, B) become more efficient and cut costs, or C) replace someone who left or is moved elsewhere. Be alert for specific developments, like those below, which can create hidden job opportunities.

1. Top management decisions create a need for new leaders and personnel not available internally
   - Oil companies that diversify into solar power create an instant need for new leadership.
   - A company acquisition results in a new executive that seeks to replace other executives or teams below her.

2. Introduction of new systems and processes
   - The introduction of digital passports or new safety procedures triggers demand for IT and security systems experts at airports and other travel hubs.

3. Opportunities arising from illness, casualty or pregnancy
   - Although a lot of companies like to retain executive female talent, pregnancy and children often lead to departures.

4. Poor management of expatriates
   - Expatriates who do not adjust well to their new nation and leave the company or are reassigned.

Why Hidden Jobs Make Sense

> **WHEN IT COMES TO TOP MANAGEMENT CHANGES, DISCRETION IS PARAMOUNT.**

Confidentiality is top priority when employers replace executives. The hiring organization may either try to hide their company name or ask executive search agencies for confidential searches. Even when turning to ads and reaching out to the public, recruiters will make every possible effort to have their client remain incognito.

When CEOs and other senior executives depart and trigger the search for a successor, it is paramount to the employer, the incumbent, and the successor to protect the image of all parties involved and to avoid leaking sensitive information.

The more discrete and confidential the search, the more attractive the opportunity becomes in the eyes of the potential successor. People value top opportunities that are confidential. Spreading information is a good way of polluting the job market and putting off high quality job candidates.

Decision-makers know that finding top talent is most important for their own success. They are under great pressure to hire and will first and foremost use their own trusted connections or employee referrals. That is their fastest and most reliable way. Involving Human Resources is a last resort and leads to a time-consuming and expensive search in the Open Job Market, where often hundreds of unsuitable job applicants blindly apply.

Moreover, some job ads are not sincere. The company already has its candidate, but it must by law or organizational rule show the position "open" to avoid discrimination lawsuits or other equal opportunity issues. This can be a terrible source of frustration for job seekers. I have coached many clients who cannot understand why they have not heard back from companies where they applied for jobs that perfectly matched their background.

Crack the Hidden Job Market Yourself

My experience has taught me that the best jobs – those that pay you well, build your career and most importantly make you happiest – are found in the Hidden Job Market. Hidden jobs are everywhere. The challenge is learning how to find them.

The Morita Method

To crack the Hidden Job Market, learn and use the Morita Method.

The Morita Method gets you in front of decision-makers. It is a systematic approach that uncovers "hidden opportunities" and gets you abundant job interviews to land multiple job offers within 120 days.

Why Job Searching In The Hidden Job Market is More Rewarding

By navigating the Hidden Job Market, you will:

- **Be in power and control:** A job search campaign in the Hidden Job Market catapults you from a dead-end job search back to a fast-track job hunt. By setting clear goals, you know what you have to do to succeed. You drive the whole job search process and negotiate your job on your terms.

- **Differentiate and market yourself as a unique solution provider:** Most job searches are hampered by unclear goals, lack of preparation, and procrastination. With The Morita Method, you diligently market your skills, experience, and reputation as a unique and innovative solution provider that maximizes opportunity while minimizing risk. Your differentiation makes competition irrelevant so that you claim uncontested leadership in your targeted areas. You define yourself as a valuable asset that companies seek to invest in.

- **Be on the fast track:** Bypass Human Resources and cut straight to the decision-maker. This way, competition is low. With your laser-sharp focus on the decision-maker's needs and well-presented solution proposals, odds are in your favor. The decision-maker will further accelerate the internal hiring process from the moment you have convinced him of your value and, as a result, you will qualify as a must hire.

- **Increase the number of on-target interviews:** The moment you systematically target your desired position in companies of your choice, the quantity and quality of your interviews will rise.

- **Land your job despite major career defects:** Everyone has a fair chance to win in the Hidden Job Market. This is especially important for job seekers who have career gaps, frequent job changes, lay-offs, and other disadvantages. As long as you have convinced the decision-maker of your execution capability and value, formal screening considerations will remain superficial concerns.

- **Gain confidence:** The proactive approach of The Morita Method brings successes that will raise your confidence. You will recognize your talents and passions, which will propel you towards landing your perfect job. Your schedule will be filled with meaningful, productive tasks that bring you closer to your declared goal, day by day.

- **Select your favorite job:** Right from the beginning, aim for at least two job offers. Instead of compromising what you want and desperately accepting the first job offer, enjoy the privilege of picking the best job offer.

Decision-makers In The Hidden Job Market

Decision-makers try different ways to find the right people. They use referrals, internal staff, word of mouth, contractors and confidential searches through recruiting agencies. If none of these approaches work, they open their needs to a broader audience through advertisement, which is when people looking for work on the Open Job Market first learn of these opportunities.

Consider how decision-makers perceive you as a candidate with a Hidden Job Market strategy.

- **The solution to their problems:** By providing proof for your performance claims, you show the decision-maker that you are best at executing the solution to her problem.

- **Having superior value:** You not only solve their problems, you are able to grow their business successfully based on your solution proposal.

- **Top on their list:** The decision-maker is considering only you and maybe a select few other candidates. You're #1. This makes it easy for them to internally sell your case to other executives, the board and Human Resources and to get you an offer quickly.

MOST IMPORTANT: By focusing on the Hidden Job Market you focus on almost all senior and top management job opportunities.

THE FIRST STEP: Read this book and learn the Morita Method.

1.2 THE NEW JOB SEARCH ECONOMICS

Marketing Yourself As A Business

The Morita Method is based on a new set of rules. To find your perfect job you first need to understand the new job search rules, which I call new job search economics. To become a successful player in the Hidden Job Market, learn the system that governs job search success.

New job search economics says that anyone in the labor market is a business. Think of yourself as a business, Me Inc. Andy Grove, CEO of Intel Corporation, once emphasized, "No matter where you work, you are not an employee. You are in business with one employer – yourself. Nobody owes you a career – you own it as a sole proprietor."[1]

Manage yourself like a business. Even employees of a company should consider themselves self-employed individuals managing their Me Inc. business. Start thinking, acting, and job searching as a Me Inc. entrepreneur from this moment forward. Fill in your first and last name — let's create your business now.

> I am _____ Corporation.

Attitude Propels Your Altitude

Develop this entrepreneurial attitude and make yourself owner of your career.

The right entrepreneurial attitude for the Morita Method is

- I only select companies I want to work for.
- I only select companies in line with my Value Proposition and Growth Agenda.
- I only select companies where I can have my perfect job.
- I only select companies willing to pay what I am worth based on value and performance.

This attitude is proactive. You initiate direct contact with decision-makers at the companies you selected.

This attitude is also contagious. It will shine through in interviews with executives, board members and other stakeholders.

Most importantly, this attitude will lead to you landing multiple job offers in 120 days.

The New Job Search Economics

In the new job search economics, you are not searching for a job. Rather, you are an investment that you are selling to a company. Therefore, target the companies and decision-makers most likely to hire you and discover opportunities invisible to you beforehand.

In the new job search economics, executive jobs are investment projects or joint ventures for your Me Inc. I see little difference between your job search and a private equity company investing in companies. Acquire your investment projects, manage and divest of them as you do with investment projects or joint ventures.

The new job search economics is about creating business opportunities, not looking for jobs. Be a business opportunity creator, not a job seeker. Your job is to use your marketing skills to define your perfect job and plan a sales campaign that presents your best value to your potential buyers. Like companies that invest in marketing and sales, you, as owner of "Me Inc.," invest in marketing yourself and selling your brand.

In the new job search economics, **value is king**. Your hiring does not depend on your skills or experience, but on the value you will generate. Therefore, you must communicate value to the decision-maker. You are recruiting a client, not a job. Therefore, understand the client's business problems and how you can solve them. Only then can you show how much value your skills and experience will generate. **Value is the** language you need to learn and master to succeed in the Hidden Job Market.

In the new job search economics, you market yourself as a unique and comprehensive solution provider. People who do not market themselves and their unique skillset become a common commodity. Common commodities sell at a low price or do not sell at all, which in this case means unemployment. What you can do best is your best guarantor to creating extraordinary value.

In the new job search economics, the bar for success has been raised. Employers expect massive value as enticement to invest in your business. Competitors are equipping themselves with the best job search coaches, strategic advisors, mentors and communication experts. Today you must perform at a higher level than you performed yesterday and assure stakeholders that tomorrow's results will be better than today's.

The new job search economics is about becoming a person in demand and job security for a lifetime.

MOST IMPORTANT: Don't beat yourself. The first sale is to yourself. Be totally convinced that with the Morita Method, you will succeed. The rest is only execution.

THE FIRST STEP: Say "I can and I will do it!"

1.3 OUTSOURCE TO GET AN EDGE

In the previous chapter, I described the new job search economics. To succeed in this market, I want you to focus on one and only one task: interviewing. You don't need to be a job search expert. You don't need to be a resume writer. Nor do you need to be a data research expert. You are an executive, and that is your expertise. This is what must shine in interviews. Communicate your value and convince decision-makers about your vision and strategy. For these other tasks, you outsource to experts. Bringing experts to do the tasks you are not good at will bring you more interviews and more job offers in less time.

Golden Rule Of The Morita Method

> **OUTSOURCE ANYTHING THAT YOU DO NOT HAVE TO DO YOURSELF.**

Outsource everything but interviews. Below are tasks I recommend outsourcing:

- Mailing List Generation *(see Chapter 3.4)*
- Value Proposition Letter and Executive Resumes *(see Chapter 4.2)*
- Mail Letter Dispatch *(see Chapter 4.3)*

Outsource to a Hidden Job Market Advisor. The Hidden Job Market Advisor is a specialist of the Hidden Job Market job. Your advisor will create your documents, distribute them to decision-makers, and prepare you for interviews. With best-in-class expertise, you get an edge during the execution of your job search campaign because you quickly overcome the two biggest hurdles for a successful job search in the Hidden Job Market: who to approach and how.

Your Hidden Job Market Advisor acts as a CEO strategic advisor. His greatest value comes from pointing you and your entire campaign to companies and decision-makers most likely to hire you as their CEO or top manager. He makes invisible top management opportunities visible. He is a job opportunity creator.

Other tasks will require data research and secretarial work. For these too, I recommend you outsource. A good Hidden Job Market Advisor will direct you towards excellent staff.

MOST IMPORTANT: The Hidden Job Market is not to be navigated alone. Recruit advisors and assistants to give your job search a significant edge.

THE FIRST STEP: Hire a Hidden Job Market Advisor with proven job search expertise and know-how to give you an invaluable edge in the job search game.

STEP 2:
DISCOVER AND DESIGN YOUR PERFECT JOB

Do you like your job? Few people do. But shouldn't you? Why not have a job that excites and energizes you? A job that brings out your best—a perfect job?

2.1 KNOW WHAT YOU WANT

Everyone wants a perfect job, but very few people know what that is. Therefore, I want to first define your perfect job, the job you really want and ultimate goal of your job search.

Knowing Your Perfect Job Is The Foundation of Your Executive Job Search in the Hidden Job Market.

Understand your passions, skills, and everything else that helps you be your best. Most people struggle mightily with this introspection, so turn to a Hidden Job Market Advisor and get the ball rolling.

How To Design Your Perfect Job:

1. Define the most crucial elements of your perfect job.
2. Order these elements in terms of priority.
3. Focus on the elements that matter most.

EXECUTIVE JOB SEARCH IN THE HIDDEN JOB MARKET

2.2 DEFINE YOUR PERFECT JOB USING THE JOB TEMPLE

When I coach my clients, I challenge them to define their perfect job by listing key elements and then prioritizing them. I have them visualize these elements as pillars that support the temple of their perfect job.

In total, I have learned there are 11 pillars:

Pillar 1. Goals

Pillar 2. Location

Pillar 3. Passion

Pillar 4. People

Pillar 5. Responsibilities

Pillar 6. Salary

Pillar 7. Skills

Pillar 8. Strengths

Pillar 9. Values

Pillar 10. Vision

Pillar 11. Working Conditions

Ignoring any of these puts you at risk of not defining your perfect job well and becoming disappointed with the job you acquire. Below I describe each pillar.

Pillar 1. Goals

Are you a CxO in a small company who wants to continue as CxO in a medium sized company? Are you a Country CFO who wants to become a Regional CFO? Maybe you are an executive at a big corporation who wants to become the CEO of a medium-sized hidden champion? The more precise your goals, the easier your search efforts will be in the Hidden Job Market and the better your communication will be with the decision-makers you connect with.

Pillar 2. Location

Where do you want to work? West Coast? East Coast? Do you need mountains, or do you prefer to be near the sea? Maybe a foreign country excites you? "Will relocate anywhere" on your executive resume is acceptable on paper, but you still have to define where exactly you want to search.

Pillar 3. Passion

Your passion is your source of strength. Without it, you do not aspire to your greatest self. Doing what you love naturally makes you a better worker. So before defining your perfect job, you need to understand what you enjoy doing and doing well. This is the basis for creating value for your employer and your employer's customers. It is also the basis for you to thrive as a business.

It probably will not surprise you to know that the majority of people are not passionate about their work. In fact, fewer than one of every four Americans have passion for their work, according to a survey conducted by Deloitte LLP in 2010.[2] Unfortunately, your job consumes 40 to 80 hours per week plus commuting. On top of that, household chores swallow the little time left over. The pervasive influence of mobile communication at work – being connected anywhere, anytime – means constant intrusion of business into your private sphere. Passion will give you a purpose that will make you more motivated, ambitious, and, most importantly, happier. You will embrace challenges because you will view them as opportunities. You will want the projects. You will want the responsibility.

So you begin by understanding yourself. Slow down and retreat to one of your favorite places to recharge your passion batteries. Switch off your mobile devices and avoid interruptions and disturbances. Unclutter your environment, untangle your mind, and optimal concentration will follow. Breaking from the daily routine and immersing yourself in a serene environment open the doors for moments of inspiration and intuition.

The underlying tenor of most literature on passion is that passion is a bonus to having a good job. But passion is your natural default setting. Denying your passion is tantamount to denying your happiness.

Pillar 4. People

Executives join brands, but leave their superiors. In fact, 80% of turnover is related to people. This pattern makes sense because most job seekers decide to join companies based on the portfolio and strengths of the company with little to no knowledge of their future colleagues. High-technology executives tend to focus too much on technology rather than the leadership team. So take the extra effort to describe in detail the profile of your ideal manager(s), peers, subordinates, board members, and key customers.

Lee Lacocca puts paramount emphasis on people: "The key to success is not information. It's people. And the kind of people I look for to fill top management spots are the eager beavers. These are the guys who try to do more than they're expected to. They're always reaching. And reaching out to the people they work with, helping them to do their jobs better. That's the way they're built. So I try to look for people with that drive.

You don't need many. With twenty-five of these guys, I could run the government of the United States."[3]

Who do you want to work with?

Pillar 5. Responsibilities

In the Hidden Job Market you need to define and negotiate your responsibilities, or co-create them with the decision-maker. Depending on what value generation, objectives and timeline both of you come to agree on, your responsibilities, decision-making authority, reporting structures and resources are up for discussion.

Pillar 6. Salary

Few companies differentiate themselves with their pay system. They should. You do as well. What constitutes fair pay for you? Pay for performance is the way to go. Your success relates to shareholder value. This is another important way to differentiate yourself in the Hidden Job Market.

Pillar 7. Skills

Your best job must draw on the skills you enjoy using most. As the American poet Robert Frost writes in *Tramps in Mudtime,* "My object in living is to unite my avocation and my vocation."[4] The ideal is to do a job you deeply love because it requires exactly the skills that give you the most joy and fulfillment. So let's find those skills.

First, list as many of your skills as you can. Then, draw the distinction between your favorite skills, your most developed and competitive skills, and skills that you believe are most lucrative. A fourth category is unique skills or a unique combination of skills. Our number one focus is the skills you love, and the intersection of all four categories is your sweet spot. Still, this skill chart must serve as a reality check. We cannot afford to only look at maximum pleasure and enjoyment in this competitive and crowded job market. To help companies excel at serving their customers, you need to be good at what you do. The better you are, the more value you can create, and the more value you can create, the more attractive you are to employers.

Pillar 8. Strengths

Never forget that you and your job are a business on two legs. The only way that your business will succeed and create excellent value is with a sustainable competitive advantage. And that sustainable competitive advantage comes from using your strengths.

There are many ways to find your strengths. Conduct a quick survey among family, friends, and colleagues that know you well. Secondly, look at your past accomplishments and identify the main attributable strengths. Thirdly, I recommend the Clifton StrengthsFinder, a paid-for on-line test that helps you find your top five strengths. For each of your top five strengths there is also a list of ten actions that help you plan your actions for applying and improving your strengths. The StrengthsFinder identified my greatest strength as connecting people and helped me execute my career as executive recruiter and job search coach.

Pillar 9. Values

Live according to your values. The word value derives from the Latin word "valere," meaning strong and healthy. Without values, people feel value-less or worthless. What is important to you? The way you spend your time and money is a strong indicator of your values. By selecting the values most important to you and selecting a job and a company that hold these values, you create ideal conditions to thrive.

Talking about values is a fuzzy topic for most people. And yet, knowing your values is imperative, because values define meaning, and therefore directly shape your vision, dreams, goals and passions.

Pillar 10. Vision

Envision your future so clearly that you can see it, feel it, taste it and smell it. It is time to think big. Think bigger, ten to one hundred times than you normally think. The Hidden Job Market rewards people with clarity of vision. Your vision is a powerful magnet attracting decision-makers and other stakeholders in your target organization.

Carlos Ghosn emphasized that one of the factors important to his spectacular turnaround of Nissan was having a simple vision. The Nissan 180 restructuring plan was about "complete revival for profitable growth," 1 million more cars sold, top level of profitability in the industry, and no debt. This vision led him to achieve top operational profit margins of 11.1% in FY03 among global automotive manufacturers.

Pillar 11. Working Conditions

Select the conditions under which you work best. Put yourself first, because when you join a system, the system will not neatly organize itself around you and your needs. A small venture is great for an entrepreneurial, do-it-yourself professional who enjoys launching new initiatives with full empowerment and quick feedback. A big multinational corporation is great for people who thrive on limited responsibility and freedom, yet seek a high degree of specialization and clear promotion possibilities and career plans. Do you want the option to work at home or are you happy going to the office every day?

When thinking about working conditions you should also consider your health. Too often people ignore or neglect their health, working at levels that cause great stress on their minds and bodies. Does your job allow you to stay healthy, fit and energized? Consider the office environment, the commute, travel and other factors that could affect your performance.

2.3 PRIORITIZE YOUR PILLARS

Now that you have defined your Job Temple, you must prioritize your pillars. List your top five job elements. Job search success requires you know what you want.

Do not expect a perfect representation of your job at your first attempt. What matters is that you keep improving. Each time you get clearer on what matters most to you, you are one step closer to your perfect job. Lloyd Blankfein, chairman and CEO of Goldman Sachs, said, "In a tough economy, or because of family pressures, you may not always be able to take a risk with a job choice. And, no doubt, we've all settled at various times. But, don't let necessity in a given moment become the excuse for a lifetime of inertia. Keep trying to get yourself to the right place."[5]

Paralysis By Analysis

Defining your Job Temple is time-consuming and demanding. Collecting and compiling all information at one time can lead to paralysis by analysis. Refining the Job Temple is an ongoing exercise. Treat it as a living document that helps guide your job search. Pillars that are easy to describe may be a sign of their priority.

Are You Convinced Of Your Perfect Job?

Does the Perfect Job you just defined reflect what you desire and deserve? Do you see yourself in your Perfect Job? Does it ring true?

> **IN THE MORITA METHOD, THE FIRST SALE IS TO YOURSELF. WOULD YOU HIRE YOURSELF?**

You can only convince others if you are convinced yourself.

Right Job, Right Career

The right job means the right career. The right career means promising and long-term success. The Morita Method not only assures clarity about your perfect job, it puts you on a successful career track and makes you a person in demand.

By carving out your perfect job, you also avoid future career bottlenecks, detours, dead-end alleys or even land mines. One ambitious global head of a specialty chemical business was a very successful executive in his mid-forties who created dominant leadership in his markets. As part of doing the job definition exercise, he realized that both his current business and that of his competitors would be too narrow with too few opportunities to progress in his career. He concluded that his perfect job was to get out of his niche and target a different, much broader sector where he was sure of solid long-term growth and upward top management opportunities.

MOST IMPORTANT: Know thyself.

THE FIRST STEP: Define together with your Hidden Job Market Advisor the pillars of your perfect job.

STEP 3:
TARGETING

3.1 IDENTIFYING INDUSTRIES AND LOCATIONS

> **DON'T SEARCH FOR JOBS. SEARCH FOR COMPANIES MOST LIKELY TO HIRE YOU.**

Targeting is about finding the companies and decision-makers most likely to hire you. To do that, you need to know the market. **To know the market, you need to research and analyze the demand patterns and job hiring trends around you.**

> **DATA DRIVES TARGETING, NOT GUT FEELINGS.**

Target your research at two levels higher than the job you want and see what trends emerge. The more closely you understand the demand and factor it into your decision-making, the better becomes your job search campaign. It becomes market-driven.

Focus On The Market

Headhunters focus on the market. They even follow the market. If hiring activities change, headhunters adapt. Do the same. Even the largest companies adapt and change. Think of consumer household names like Siemens, Toshiba and Hitachi. Today, they are energy companies. Qiagen, a leading German biotech company, started out as a chemistry company, became a biology company, then an engineering company, a medically oriented company for hospitals and clinics and finally a software company. Panasonic's global headquarter for purchasing and Sharp's TV business both moved from Osaka, Japan, to Singapore and Shanghai, respectively.

> **UNLESS YOU FOLLOW YOUR MARKET, YOU WILL NOT REACH YOUR TARGET.**

Hidden Job Market Advisor as CEO Strategic Advisor

This is true. The Hidden Job Market is an ocean of hidden job opportunities. To navigate through this ocean and secure the hidden job which best matches your vision, passion, values, talents and experience, you need the Hidden Job Market Advisor. The targeting task requires the Hidden Job Market Advisor to act like a CEO Strategic Advisor. Because he identifies existing hidden opportunities inside companies, and that he creates hidden jobs for you, he plays a critical role in guiding you to where your chances of getting hired are highest.

> **MANY EXECUTIVES ARE LOST IN AN OCEAN OF POSSIBILITIES.**

Targeting

Targeting is done at four different levels:

1. Target countries.
2. Target "hot spots" (such as states, regions or towns).
3. Target industries.
4. Target jobs.

Relevant statistics can show you the benefits of making smart targeting decisions. It is useful to make decisions based on technical data, but not always necessary. The strategic divisions of Honda Motor Corporation and Mitsubishi Heavy Industries built their own aircraft which gave birth to the commercial aircraft businesses in Japan and triggered demand for aircraft industry experts across the whole value chain.

Ask people who know the inside scoop of the local employment and job trend scene.

1. Target Countries

First, select your favorite country, then your favorite state or region, and then your favorite town.

In 2012, there were 48 countries in the world with less unemployment than the United States. The unemployment in countries as different as Thailand, Vietnam, Switzerland, Qatar and Norway was below 3%. You can offset economic downturns in one country by searching in booming economies in which hiring is in full swing.

2. Target Specific Hot Spots

During the so-called Big Recession from 2007 to 2011 in the United States, nationwide employment fell 5%, losing 6.5 million jobs. However, 182 economic hot spots grew during the same period.

Hot spots are economic powerhouses confined to states, regions and cities with above-average growth rates and reliable demand for labor.

For example, from 2007 to 2011 Williston, ND, grew 79%, Dickinson, ND, grew 26%, Raymondville, TX, grew 23%, and Dodge City, KS, grew 17%. Larger cities added jobs as well, such as Houston, TX, with 41,500 jobs, and New Orleans, LA, with 17,500.

3. Target Specific Industries

Example: Specific industries in the United States

You need to target industries. No more than three. One is best. Your job search odds are best in industries that have been growing over the last four years. Consider some of the below industry hot spots for targeting.

For the information industry, Napa, CA, at 13%, and Logan, UT, at 8%, were the two top hot spots. For the manufacturing industry, Casper, WY, at 12%, and Tulsa, OK, at 9% took this title. For private education, Honolulu, (HI), at 9%, and Phoenix-Mesa-Glendale, AZ, at 7%, were tops.

Or consider California. Construction lost 336,000, or 37%, of its jobs, whereas manufacturing lost 204,000, or 14%, of its jobs. Yet even within manufacturing, computer and peripheral equipment manufacturing grew 12%, communication equipment manufacturing grew 15% and medical equipment and supplies grew 5%.

Finally, let's look at industry growth rates. In 2011, the industry hiring most was mining. Between 2000 and 2011, the industry growing the most was grant-making foundations. In fact, grant-making foundations, such as the Ford Foundation or the Bill & Melinda Gates Foundation, have been the fastest-growing industry in the United States over the last ten years and are a promising area to uncover hidden jobs.

> **DATA DRIVES YOUR DECISIONS,
> NOT GUT FEELINGS.**

Let data help you decide to stay in or switch industries as well as to stay or relocate, and if relocating, to which country, state or town. Finding your perfect job is most effective in hot spots where jobs are easiest to find. In 2012, Dickinson, for example, had 1,500 open jobs and 1.5% unemployment.

Example: Growing industries in selected countries

For executives interested in international opportunities, consider the following:

- **United Arab Emirates:** aviation and retailing
- **Malaysia:** healthcare tourism and biotechnology
- **Japan:** jet and aircraft manufacturing
- **Australia:** gas industry
- **India:** mobile data services
- **Mexico:** automotive manufacturing
- **Germany:** environmental technologies
- **China:** electric bicycles

In fact, Mexico is becoming an automotive manufacturing powerhouse with Aguascalientes being the hot spot. Mexico increased its share of North American automotive jobs from 27% in 2000 to 40% in 2014, attracting $19 billion in foreign direct investment. Daimler decided to cut jobs in Germany and move production of its most popular transport utility Sprinter to North America, most likely Mexico. The VW luxury brand Audi moved its Q5 production from Germany not to the United States, but Mexico. Why? Mexico is the country with the highest number of free-trade agreements, making it the ideal location to invest in to produce and export automobiles worldwide. And hundreds of automotive suppliers need to follow the footsteps of car manufacturers. It is no surprise automotive executives are in huge demand in Mexico and will be for quite a while.

4. Target Specific Jobs

Target specific jobs or job categories. This sounds like common sense, but a lot of job seekers struggle with naming their target job correctly.

Let me give you some examples about the effectiveness of different types of targeting.

Untargeted:

- Something in the IT industry
- I want to be a social entrepreneur.

Targeted to some degree:

- A general manager job in a semiconductor company
- A turn-around executive in Fortune 500 companies

Highly targeted:

- A general manager position in an American analog company in Japan with a size of 1 to 20 employees
- A social community and service manager at a Top 100 grant-making foundation in California
- A general manager for a U.S. or European Tier 2 automotive supplier in Mexico

Validating Specific Jobs Using Job Trends

Target specific jobs and discover their job trends. Job trends about industries are not extremely useful; you need to get down to specific jobs and determine the extent to which they are in demand. Government employment agencies or industry associations usually have such information. Although the number of IT jobs as a whole is declining, a closer look at specific niches in the IT industry reveals strong long-term demand for Big Data jobs and more specifically jobs for Big Data architects. Big Data architects are a promising target in the Hidden Job Market.

Highest Job Searching Odds

Find industries in or near your area that are growing now and have been growing over the last four years. You fish where the fish are, so job search where the jobs are.

MOST IMPORTANT: Investigate. Focus. Then, fish.

THE FIRST STEP: Select a highly targeted job in your favorite location.

3.2 FINDING HIDDEN INFORMATION

The Research Meeting

Research meetings are field research for the sake of collecting information about your target job, company, or industry. They are a systematic way of networking in the Hidden Job Market to get more information about your industry before you contact or meet the decision-makers. Research meetings are beneficial to all professionals, but they are particularly useful to those planning a career change.

Most executives are familiar with market research as a way to get what they need to know to move forward with business. They are usually at a loss, however, on how to find information on hidden jobs. This is why research meetings play an important role.

When To Conduct Research Meetings

Use research meetings when planning your career and job search. Before you decide on a specific job or professional field, conducting three to five research meetings will clarify whether your target job or industry is worth pursuing. On the other hand, for job changers who are clear about the type of job they want, research meetings are a valuable resource to help you ascertain the decision-maker's priorities, needs and interests, and therefore help you prepare for interviews.

The Power To Know

As Aristotle Onassis said, "The secret of business is knowing something nobody else knows."[6]

Research meetings will help you:

- Gain clarity and insight about the real nature and specifics of your target jobs and industries
- Build your network in your target industries and companies
- Better understand your target organization's hiring needs
- Develop your ideas and arguments for the hiring interview
- Discover your strengths and weaknesses that address hidden hiring needs
- Obtain first-hand salary information to negotiate the best deal for yourself

With Whom To Arrange Research Meetings

> **AVOID PEOPLE WITH THE POWER TO HIRE YOU.**

Avoid people with the power to hire you. You only want to target these people when you are clear on what they want and that you can give it. Prematurely contacting people with the power to hire you is a frequent mistake of Hidden Job Market searchers.

Choose incumbents of the job you are targeting or experts in the industry you are investigating.

Persistence And Tenacity

Persistence pays off when trying to make appointments of any kind, especially when asking your interviewee for a favor. This task often requires creativity, persuasion, and persistence.

According to research performed by the National Sales Executive Association:

- 2% of sales are made on the first contact.
- 3% of sales are made on the second contact.
- 5% of sales are made on the third contact.
- 10% of sales are made on the fourth contact.
- 80% of sales are made on the fifth through twelfth contacts.

Research shows that even top sales people contact their customer on average 5-6 times before making the sale.

The lesson here is: If you fail, keep trying and learn from your previous mistakes.

How To Arrange Research Meetings

Research meetings involve you requesting information and time, often from complete strangers. This is not an insignificant favor.

Appeal to them by remembering that people enjoy :

1. Talking about their passions and their life.
2. Helping those in need.

Ask yourself, "Why should this prospective interviewee meet me?" Having a common acquaintance is of great help. But sometimes even that may not be enough. What can you do to get your meeting quickly and move forward with your fast-track job search?

Create "Why-not?" Opportunities To Connect

Then ask, "What is the easiest and least disruptive way to meet this person for 15 minutes?" Time is money, but even a busy executive can usually afford up to 15 minutes if you propose both a specific time and a venue where he cannot but think to himself, "Why not?" Such "Why not?" opportunities arise, for example, before or after morning brunches or lunch meetings, at executive or golf clubs lounges, PR events and tradeshows, during taxi rides or on shuttle buses, or even at the office.

Prepare Questions To Make The Most Out Of A Research Meeting

The research meeting is all about engaging your interviewee in a meaningful conversation to gain the information, advice, and insight you seek. Use pointed and engaging questions to lead the person to share as much as they can.

Have your top three questions ready.

Know exactly what to ask and how to ask. Remember, you are asking for the person's time. In addition, you may need her again. Therefore, you must be prepared to make the most out of this short interview. The questions in Appendix 3 can help you.

How To Analyze Research Meeting Data

It is critical to evaluate your accumulated data for each target job or industry. Common or similar responses from different people for one chosen career path indicate patterns relevant to your future job or industry and, more importantly, hiring needs. You also become aware of gaps in skills and experience you may have, as well as early warning signs of mismatches and possible red flags.

Mistakes To Avoid At Research Meetings

- **Asking for jobs:** The most common mistake associated with research meetings is to ask your meeting partner for a job or how to get jobs. Asking this turns the research meeting into an ambush interview that the interviewee never agreed to. Ambushing your interviewee makes her suspicious and reluctant to share information or her time with you any further.

- **Bringing your executive resume:** Another frequent mistake is to bringing your executive resume to the research meeting and giving it to your meeting partner. Your interviewee could feel abused and is most likely to forward your executive resume to Human Resources, if anyone, thereby bringing your Hidden Job Market initiative to an abrupt end. Never bring an executive resume; don't even mention it since you are solely meeting for the sake of learning information, not gaining immediate employment.

- **Failing to follow up the interview:** Send a written thank-you note containing your contact details to the person you interviewed. A thank-you note provides another opportunity for you to share information, especially things you forgot to mention during the interview. You will learn more about proper interview follow-up in Chapter 5.3.

MOST IMPORTANT: Be confident in your questions and your pursuit.

THE FIRST STEP: Write down your top three questions for a research meeting.

3.3 DIRECT MAIL

Introduction To Direct Mailing

When was the last time you received a letter with your name and the sender's name handwritten on the envelope? It's pretty rare today, no? What would you do if you did receive such a letter, even if you did not recognize the name? Wouldn't you open it and at least glance at the content?

That is why the Morita Method recommends contacting prospective companies by direct mail. Yes, old-fashioned regular mail through the post office. Direct mail is the best way to get enough interviews to receive multiple job offers in 120 days.

Timing Is Crucial

The most important task for an effective Hidden Job Market search is talking to decision-makers.

The ideal timing for talking to decision-makers is shortly before a job opportunity materializes. Those who have already talked to decision-makers and presented their value propositions have secured themselves for being considered for a new opening.

Direct mail in the Hidden Job Market solves the problem of timing because it gives you assurance of **meeting** enough **decision-makers** to land multiple job offers, out of which you select your favorite job.

> **THE MOST IMPORTANT ELEMENT OF YOUR EXECUTIVE JOB SEARCH CAMPAIGN IS REACHING DECISION-MAKERS, IDEALLY BEFORE THEY HAVE AN OPENING.**

Timing is crucial. Your core message must arrive at exactly the right time. The timing will be wrong for the vast majority of target companies.

However, the timing is right for numerous target companies that will have a need for you.

Direct Mail Gives You Certainty

With direct mail, you can, in less than two weeks, complete a snail mail campaign that has reached as many as 5,000 decision-makers.

For you, the active job seeker, direct mail provides certainty: It is the only way to accomplish your goal of securing at least two offers within 120 days.

The reason that this is successful is that you can increase the number of outgoing letters until the odds are in your favor of getting 25 interviews, which in turn gives you a good chance to win at least two job offers. This is why direct mail is a targeted marketing machine that you should use in the Hidden Job Market to uncover hidden jobs. No other job search channel offers such certainty.

Direct Mail Puts You On The Fast Track

Direct mail has the dramatic effect of accelerating your job search in a short four-month period. It is like a catapult. It is a tailored mass-production machine built for the Hidden Job Market. A correctly executed direct mailing campaign hits decision-makers, gives you interviews, and leads to job offers. This is a powerful career-enhancement program you cannot neglect.

Use Direct Mail For Your Job Search

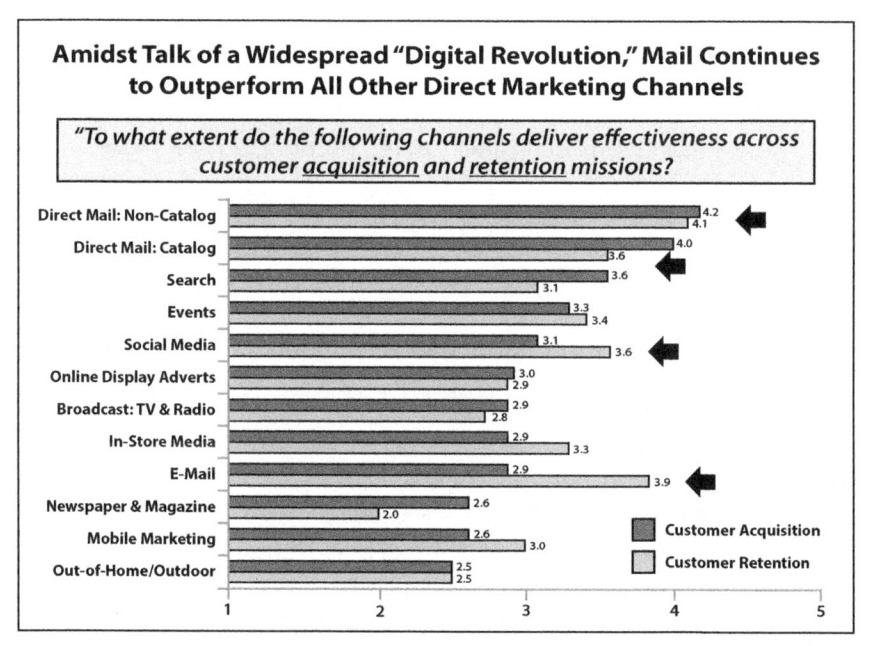

Amidst Talk of a Widespread "Digital Revolution," Mail Continues to Outperform All Other Direct Marketing Channels

"To what extent do the following channels deliver effectiveness across customer acquisition and retention missions?"

Channel	Customer Acquisition	Customer Retention
Direct Mail: Non-Catalog	4.2	4.1
Direct Mail: Catalog	3.6	4.0
Search	3.6	3.1
Events	3.3	3.4
Social Media	3.1	3.6
Online Display Adverts	3.0	2.9
Broadcast: TV & Radio	2.9	2.8
In-Store Media	2.9	3.3
E-Mail	2.9	3.9
Newspaper & Magazine	2.6	2.0
Mobile Marketing	2.6	3.0
Out-of-Home/Outdoor	2.5	2.5

Source: Winterberry Group, 2010, Printed with Permission.

For those who consider direct mail as anachronistic and expensive, be advised that despite the digital marketing revolution, classic mail continues to be the number one direct marketing medium *(see Graph)*.

***The advantages of my direct mailing approach
in the Hidden Job Market are:***

1. **Direct mail enables you to reach more people in less time than any other technique.** It provides you almost unlimited job search power and the most flexibility in the number of people you reach. Crafting a compelling Value Proposition Letter (see Chapter 4.2) and delivering it to thousands of decision-makers at once makes direct mail more effective than other job channels.

2. **Direct mail with the Morita Method offers fantastic Return On Investment**, out-performing other job search methods or career enhancing programs.

3. **Direct mail is personal.** The great practitioner, Stan Rapp, called it "intimate advertising." Marketing expert Denison Hatch confesses: "No other medium enables a marketer to become so immediately close to a prospect as the direct mail letter – that emotion-laden, me-to-you correspondence that allows you to fire your message of any length at point-blank range in the privacy of an office."[8]

4. **You do not need a network to approach decision-makers.** This is particularly relevant if you are exploring new geographic areas where you do not have contacts.

5. **It's fast. Remember, we want a job offer in 120 days.** By starting your campaign with direct mail, you are more likely to achieve this goal.

6. **Direct mail is measurable and predictable. You can test, improve and statistically predict the results.** If you need 25 first interviews to get at least two offers, you can make a simple calculation: With an estimated positive response rate x, you need y number of letters.

7. **A low percentage of job seekers use direct mailing.** Less than 3% of executives use direct mail for job search. Your Value Proposition Letter will have limited or even no competition at the recipient's desk.

MOST IMPORTANT: Direct mail is a targeted marketing weapon that enables you **to reach** more people in less time than any other technique.

THE FIRST STEP: Build your mailing list by reading the next chapter.

3.4 BUILDING YOUR MAILING LIST

Estimate at least two weeks to build a successful direct mailing list. Creating the mailing list is a task outsourced to a data researcher, and, while waiting for your mailing list, you can conduct other tasks in your job search campaign, such as writing your Value Proposition Letter and executive resume *(see Chapter 4.2)*.

The 50-40-10 Rule

Success in the Hidden Job Market hinges 50% on your mailing list, 40% on your Value Proposition Letter and 10% on your copy. I ignore the copy, because standard-sized executive letterhead and envelopes are all you need. In creative industries, such as entertainment, media or advertising, the importance of the copy may rise significantly.

The Mailing List Is The Heart Of Your Campaign

To reach decision-makers, you need an effective mailing list. Your mailing list is a database, usually kept in a spreadsheet that comprises of all the decision-makers at the companies you are targeting.

The database will include the company name and address as well as the name of the executive or owner.

The list is at the heart of your marketing efforts. If you cannot reach the people with the power to hire you, you cannot sell your solution.

> **NO MAILING LIST,
> NO INTERVIEWS.**

Find And Select The Right Lists

Unless you are searching a new field of industry or service, one that is too narrow, marginal and specialized or one that is never publicly recorded, the chances are high that there already exist the lists you want. Some of these are free, some are not. Your first challenge is finding these lists. Your second and bigger challenge is selecting the right lists.

The Advantage Of Using Lists

Lists save you a lot of research time. In many cases, lists will include:

1. Company name
2. Executive's name
3. Company address
4. Executive's contact details including telephone number and email address.

Imagine building a list of hundreds of companies in the elderly care market. Imagine searching the yellow pages for companies and their telephone numbers, or the internet for homepages and email addresses. And don't forget to compile all of these records into a structured, workable list.

Boost your productivity multiple times by taking advantage of existing lists.

How To Find Company Lists

You will find lists where large or specialized networks exist, convene or communicate. Below are places where lists are likely to exist:

Lists Of Networks:

- Industry associations
- Associations of any kind matching your search parameters
- Chambers of commerce
- NPO member companies
- Tradeshows, seminars, round-tables
- Conferences and conventions
- University or MBA career centers
- Corporate alumni clubs

Selecting Decision-makers

The targeted executives should be two levels higher in the organizational hierarchy than your target job. If you are aiming for a functional CxO position, aim for the CEO. If you want to become CEO, address the Chairman of a public company or the family owners of a privately held medium-sized organization. If you want to become Regional Head of Treasury for a global company, address the Global Head of Treasury or the headquarter CFO.

Determine The Size of Your Mailing List

Determining the size of your mailing list requires a series of judgment calls regarding criteria. The table on the following page.

TACTICS IN DETERMINING MAILING LIST SIZE	
Criteria	*Number of letters*
Is the area and target industry growing and stable?	Fewer letters
Is the economy strong?	Fewer letters
Is my value proposition compelling and in demand?	Fewer letters
Am I switching industries?	More letters
Am I searching locally?	Fewer letters
Am I searching internationally?	More letters

Higher-pay executives – above $200,000 – need to send more letters. Lower-pay executives need to send less because there are fewer higher-pay positions available than lower-pay positions. For cross-border job searches which involve a different language and culture, send more than for domestic career transitions. The attrition rate will be higher because of language and cultural barriers.

Not Enough Target Companies?

Most executives underestimate the number of target companies. Expect this number to be in the thousands – yes, thousands!

This is not a trivial number. However, the Morita Method has a solution.

Get Your Mailing List Fast

The Morita Method understands that operating alone in your search lowers your chances of success. Go the fast track and lean on your Hidden Job Market Advisor, who will help you compile an immaculate mailing list.

Lists belong in the hands of experts. Good lists are never good enough. To have an effective job search, you need perfect lists.

> **THE DIFFERENCE BETWEEN AN EXCELLENT LIST AND A GOOD LIST IS SUCCESS OR FAILURE.**

Getting accurate data can cut the costs of your search by 50% or more. Think about your job search campaign as an investment project: only the expert can assure a successful campaign and offer you remarkable Return on Investment.

Reducing Opportunity Cost For Unemployed Executives

Despite these initial costs incurred by direct mail, the Morita Method job search campaign actually reduces the costs of unemployment. Job searching is extraordinarily expensive. For a $200,000 executive, a day of unemployment costs $548 ($200,000 DIV 365). This is worth a night at a five-star hotel in New York or London. Executives take on average 10 months to find a job according to the U.S. Bureau of Labor, and these 10 months represent $164,383 of lost income.

Since the Morita Method shrinks your job search to 120 days and your period of unemployment from ten to four months, your costs of not making the money you deserve dramatically decreases. For a $200,000 executive, the cost saving after deducting the cost of the job search campaign is about $90,000. Not only do you cut your job search time in half, you stand to gain multiple times the initial investments of the Morita Method campaign. This return on investment represents irresistible value for the money-conscious executive.

MOST IMPORTANT: The mailing list is your market. 50% of your direct mail campaign success hinges on building the right mailing list.

THE FIRST STEP: You do not need to master building lists of thousands of companies, but you need to master delegating this task to your Hidden Job Market Advisor.

STEP 4:

COMMUNICATING YOUR VALUE

4.1 CREATE AN IRRESISTIBLE UNIQUE VALUE PROPOSITION

Let us summarize where we are in your job search so far. We have defined your dream job and a plan on how to get it. We have identified your target companies and prepared a mailing list to contact them. Now, we need to decide what you offer your target companies. I call this your Unique Value Proposition.

What Is A Unique Value Proposition?

Your Unique Value Proposition shares to the decision-maker the unique value you offer her company and is intended to convince her that she should meet you urgently.

The best Unique Value Propositions are made in partnership with your Hidden Job Market Advisor.

Value Proposition Builder

How To Create A Compelling Unique Value Proposition

Business Issue: Select the business issue or category of problems that you have previously solved. Focus on an issue that causes stress to the decision-maker.

BUSINESS ISSUE OR CATEGORY OF PROBLEMS THAT YOU HAVE PREVIOUSLY SOLVED	
Focus on an issue that causes stress to the decisionmaker.	
Sales Revenue Market Share Net Profits/Margin Net Operating Profit/Margin Lifetime Customer Value Dividends Return On Investment EBIDTA	Time To Market Lead Time Delivery Time Response Time Throughput Time Turnaround Time
Operating Costs Cost Per Hire Fixed / Variable Costs Labor Costs	Quality Customer Satisfaction Employee Satisfaction/Engagement
Productivity Machine Utilization Job Attendance Rate	Compliance Risk Exposure

Key Performance Indicator: Decide *what* to measure. Select an indicator that shows how well you have solved a business issue.

There are four main ways to show value:

1. By making more money through increasing sales revenue, profits or reducing costs.
2. By increasing quality and ultimately customer satisfaction.
3. By saving time.
4. By avoiding or reducing risk.

KPI Performance Leap: Measure your value with your KPI. Portray a leap in performance or productivity made possible through you and your solution.

Increase Your Value To Achieve The Best Version Of Yourself

Increase your value. To be an executive at the edge and create demand for yourself, innovate to offer irresistible value. Executives offering inferior value become a commodity nobody wants. You on the other hand, create uncontested demand for yourself. Carve out that best version of yourself and claim uncontested leadership for what you do or want to do before somebody else does.

Unique Value Proposition Template

To build a Unique Value Proposition, use the Unique Value Proposition template:

> I helped (target decision-makers or target companies) to improve or solve (business issue) by (Key Performance Indicator) in (period of time).

Let us look at several examples of Unique Value Propositions.

My value proposition is to help international executives find their perfect job in half the time.

An elder CFO in the U.S. market I coached used the following Unique Value Proposition:

> I help medium sized Italian subsidiaries in the USA achieve a 20% net profit increase within 18 months and drive a continuous cost reduction culture satisfying multiple stakeholders.

Another client of mine, a wireless telecommunications General Manager, stated the following Unique Value Proposition:

I helped transform wireless telecommunications companies into data-centric market leaders and achieve up to 50% of revenue from data services in 12 months.

You may create different value propositions if you are targeting different industries or target locations. Your Unique Value Proposition is compelling when it makes the decision-maker think or say, "Tell me more."

Talk Results, Not Process

The most common mistake of job seekers is to tell the decision-maker who you are and what you do at your current employer. Instead of years of experience, tell your legacy. Instead of describing your skills, tell your accomplishments.

Second, don't create Unique Value Propositions with companies in mind, but with decision-makers in mind. Make your Unique Value Propositions relevant and specific, enticing and compelling.

Third, people often forget the element of time. By adding time to your value proposition, you make it more powerful.

Value Is In The Eye Of The Beholder

Value is in the eye of the beholder, not yours. When preparing your Unique Value Proposition, first think about shareholder value, then the value perceived, expressed and measured by the different stakeholders you are meeting. This is nothing new. The entire enterprise solution industry is centered on end-user value.

An important challenge of the Hidden Job Market is inconsistent value perceptions of different stakeholders in the same company or the same division. What constitutes good value for the leader of the CEO selection committee and board members may appear unrealistic or out of touch with the business needs perceived by the Senior Vice President of Sales.

A universal solution may not exist, meaning you must always customize your Unique Value Proposition for different interviewers.

What Happens If You Are New To An Industry?

Let us assume that you have no track record or you just changed industries. Or you specialize in a new niche requiring a different skill set from the ones you have. Conduct research meetings *(Chapter 3.2)* with incumbents, managers or consultants in your target field. Find out what top and average first-year performance is and how quickly you can learn and catch up. Then select your KPI to measure and create an impressive yet realistic Unique Value Proposition.

What Happens If You Are Not A Top Value Creator?

Now, what should you do if you are not a top performing professional? Decision-makers give priority to excellent talent. There is a premium for excellence in terms of cost, performance and quality.

The good news is that the Hidden Job Market is vast. The pool of good but unknown small and medium-sized enterprises, so-called hidden champions, offers abundant opportunities.

Target booming areas of the Hidden Job Market where your skills are scarce and value creators are in great demand. Employers are eager to hire, even if the skill a value creator is offering is only mediocre.

Hunting opportunities is easiest where companies are desperate. You therefore want to search for employers who have big demands and desperately need solution providers.

Accept that there is nothing wrong with being an average performer. Ordinary people create extraordinary results. It is very important that you be honest and always communicate your true value without embellishing projections. Do not create false expectations. But equally important is to show how you plan to become a top performing professional in the future. If you are still struggling to be persuasive, assess the skills at which you are best. Focusing on are best at or will be best at these skills can remove the problem associated with being average.

Your Unique Value Proposition is the core element of your job search campaign.

MOST IMPORTANT: The ultimate goal of a strong value proposition is to get a prospective employer to think, "Hmm… That's interesting. I MUST learn more."

THE FIRST STEP: Use the Unique Value Proposition template to create your Unique Value Proposition.

4.2 COMMUNICATING YOUR UNIQUE VALUE PROPOSITION

Once you have your Unique Value Proposition, you must communicate it to the decision-makers on your mailing list. Therefore, the next step is to prepare your Value Proposition Letter.

The Value Proposition Letter

The Value Proposition Letter is a powerfully crafted letter that communicates your value to a company. It is your first contact with key decision-makers and is intended to convince them they should meet you.

What The Value Proposition Letter Does

A decision-maker is interested in what you can do – for her! That is why you must communicate your Unique Value Proposition. The Value Proposition Letter informs the key decision-maker of your value in 60 seconds. It's like a billboard on the road or a flyer on the street, an advertisement for your best product – you! It answers the decision-maker's overriding question: "What can this person do for me?" and also, "How can I contact this person?"

How To Craft A Value Proposition Letter

Because the reader must be able to consume all of the letter's information in less than one minute, and because it is intended to convince the reader that you are someone he or she should meet, all Value Proposition Letters have the same template.

Beginning

First, you need to grip the reader's attention with an effective opening line. I recommend you begin with a question like:

    Do you need _____?

Does your main client/project need _____?

Would you like to/some _____?

Find a question where the other side will spontaneously say "yes."

Main Text

Present your Unique Value Proposition, and then provide three accomplishments in bullet-point format that underline your Unique Value Proposition.

Ending

Explain your current status and indicate your total compensation.

Also, do not forget to finish with a P.S. that includes a reply mechanism, such as a call for action to contact you, and point to a website if you have one.

Sample Value Proposition Letters can be seen in Appendix 2.

Size Of Letter

Aim for 150 words, no more. Remember, the decision-maker should be able to read your letter in one minute.

Test And Edit Your Letter

Test your Value Proposition Letter. Without testing, you risk a very poor response rate.

Seek objections. Seek criticism. Consult not only your Hidden Job Market Advisor, but also people you know in the industry. Better to have people you trust tell you it stinks than to have the decision-maker think so and throw it away. Going through at least 10 to 20 drafts is normal. Craft your letter carefully, but read it aloud at that 60 second pace. Every word counts.

Avoid any words or expressions with potentially negative or pretentious meanings or connotations. For example, "to save" is a negative word. Use "to increase" instead.

Your letter must succeed upon its first reading. It must make you look good, no ifs, ands, or buts. If your readers hesitate at all, then modify your letter. The goal is to have the reader want to hear more.

Disclose Your Executive Compensation

I insist that you include your current compensation in the letter. In the Morita Method, you do not want to pursue leads that in the end do not satisfy your Job Temple requirements. Stating your salary allows YOU, and not the hiring company, to define compensation benchmarks.

I have seen a lot of unnecessary interviews and offer letters because both parties are unnecessarily late in touching the critical topic of executive compensation. Put it on the agenda early.

Changing Jobs And Industries

The Value Proposition Letter is most effective for people aiming at the same industry, title, or responsibilities. You can still use it for extreme change, provided you can substantiate your claims with transferable skills or unique assets such as patents as well as customer connections. The more change involved in your career transition, the less value you showcase and the less effective the Value Proposition Letter becomes. Circumstances like these make the hiring of a Hidden Job Market Advisor all the more important.

What About Executive Resumes?

Although everyone assumes executive resumes are the way to impress decision-makers and land first interviews, I actually put much more emphasis on Value Proposition Letters. Your time should be devoted more to these than executive resumes. However, many companies still expect executive resumes so they cannot be dismissed. I recommend you outsource executive resume writing to your Hidden Job Market Advisor.

Why Outsource Your Executive Resume?

First off, you are not writing a regular resume, but an executive resume. Executive resumes have a certain format so that your best skills and accomplishments shine. Assuming your Hidden Job Market Advisor knows the industry you are searching, he will have written thousands of executive resumes already for people like you. Most jobseekers cannot prepare highly customized content that gets the desired reaction from a decision-maker. Your Hidden Job Market Advisor, however, is an expert.

Most executive resumes provide too much irrelevant information that only distracts the decision- maker. Your executive resume should focus only on your career history that matters to the decision-maker. An excellent Hidden Job Market Advisor will select these items and present them on executive resume real estate that showcases you at your best.

Having well-laid-out executive resume enables the reader to capture in 10 seconds the essence of your value and background.

The Executive Resume Must Show Accomplishments That Project Value To The Decision-maker.

Your Hidden Job Market Advisor will design an executive resume that shows accomplishments that:

    1. Match or exceed the needs of the decision-maker

    2. Override the decision-maker's hiring procrastination

    3. Define what you do best and what value you generated for previous employers

The Hidden Job Market Advisor will customize your executive resume so that it answers the following questions:

1. Are my accomplishments aligned with my value proposition and of value to my target organizations?
2. Do my accomplishments show the value I created for past employers effectively?

Style, Form And Layout – The HOW

The design of an executive resume varies with industry and country. As a Hidden Job Market Advisor, I help executives make informed decisions about executive resume creation. In addition to providing American, English, German, Japanese, French and Italian resumes, I often write executive resumes that are accepted at any company that operates internationally.

Executive Resume Writing From The Hidden Job Market Advisor

Before the Hidden Job Market Advisor starts rewriting the whole executive resume, he reviews the executive resume written by you.

Let's take an example of an executive from Germany in his mid-40s who plans to transition out of a top executive role at a utility to an international CEO role:

- The executive resume was almost a direct translation in content, form and style from the German to English, projecting the image of a German executive. For example, the head of the executive resume featured a photo, which is common in many European style executive resumes, followed by private details. Also, the executive resume mentioned Chief Technical Officer as job title, although in truth the candidate has had a CEO-type role for four years.

- The format of the executive resume was typical of a middle management project manager, not a top manager. The executive resume lacked sales performance information and was instead full of technical details projecting the image of a "techie."

- The executive resume was historical, stating what was done without highlighting key accomplishments. Consider that even though he listed 30 accomplishments, it was unclear which were the most important. The executive's work experience started at age 31, with everything before then attributed to university education.

- The executive resume size was 7 pages, with 1 page dedicated entirely to education.

Overall, this executive resume suggested the candidate as a perfect CTO for utilities in Germany, but not a good match for international companies and roles. Thus, executive recruiters predominantly proposed such roles, even though the candidate stated clearly that high-tech manufacturers were the goal. For the same reason, a direct mail campaign is bound to fail because of misalignment between the CEO Value Proposition and CTO-type executive resume.

A Hidden Job Market Advisor would rewrite an executive resume with the following in mind:

- An executive resume that clearly mentions CEO or General Manager as the target position.

- The photo and private details at the top of the resume executive resume is replaced with a leadership summary, core competencies and skills for a CEO position.

- The format and style are changed from middle manager to top executive to produce an "international executive resume" suitable for executive jobs worldwide.

- The number of accomplishments is reduced to nine and quantified. Plus, unnecessary technical jargon is removed.

- Each accomplishment underlines important CEO traits, such as sales, team building, international business development, and product development breakthroughs.

- The executive resume is rewritten to prominently feature international business experience.

- Education is reduced to one quarter of a page.

- What was previously featured as PhD academic research was in reality industrial research as a project leader with top industrial companies where the executive was granted a PhD on the side. Thus, instead of five years in academia, the executive resume featured five years of leading-edge industrial R&D experience.

MOST IMPORTANT: The Value Proposition Letter is what gets you interviews; the executive resume is an auxiliary tool.

THE FIRST STEP: Write and test your Value Proposition Letter.

4.3 MAILING YOUR DOCUMENTS

Now that you have your Value Proposition Letter and executive resume ready, your next step is to disseminate these documents to all the decision-makers on your mailing list.

Bulk Mailing Is More Difficult Than You Think

Mailing thousands of letters requires logistics and experience. You must simultaneously manage several processes. It is a tricky task and is more demanding than most people realize.

The Smarter Way – Outsource Your Mass Mailing

Let me repeat the Golden Rule of the Morita Method: Outsource anything that you do not have to do yourself. Mass mailing is a routine task to outsource.

Dispatch – Do It All At Once

You must send all your letters at once. Do not send batches, beginning with the companies you really want to join or some other strategy. Anything other than one mass mail risks your 120-day deadline.

Timing Of Your Mailing Campaign

Your direct mailing campaign comes first, not last. Avoid using other job search techniques and then resorting to direct mailing as a last means. This is a waste of your time and is therefore lost potential income you could have earned from joining a suitable company.

Benefits Of Direct Mail

Beginning your job search campaign with direct mail has several positive side effects. It requires several exercises that bring clarity of action and certainty of results. Working simultaneously on your value and your targets are essential tasks. The earlier you know them, the better your job search.

Merits Of Outsourcing Mailing

The main benefit of outsourcing mailing is saving time.

MOST IMPORTANT: Outsource mass mailing.

THE FIRST STEP: Outsource to your Hidden Job Market Advisor.

STEP 5:
MEETING THE DECISION-MAKER

Where You Are With The Morita Method

We are now at the stage where you have mailed your Value Proposition Letters to your target companies. During the following four weeks, expect the bulk of your responses, which will include several invitations for interviews. Congratulations, it is now time to meet the decision-makers of 25 different companies.

5.1 PEAK PERFORMANCE INTERVIEWING IN THE HIDDEN JOB MARKET

Interviewing In Line With The Morita Method

It is not the best candidate who gets the job, but the one who interviews best.

Interviewing is THE job search activity in which you must excel.

Be Prepared For An Interview Marathon

The Morita Method aims to acquire at least two job offers and therefore assumes you will need 25 first interviews. Add to this second and third interviews, and you find yourself in an interview marathon.

You must be prepared, because:

- The interview period for your campaign is a short window of opportunity.
- Interview preparation and follow-up requires attention to detail, a lot of time and persistency.
- You need to discover and collect the hidden issues plaguing the decision-maker and other stakeholders, enabling you to move forward and drive the whole process to finalizing an offer.
- You must customize your core message to each executive you meet.

Although all this may sound daunting, the Morita Method assures that you are prepared.

Ideal Conditions

The Morita Method creates ideal conditions for you to succeed in interviews because:

- Outsourcing all other job search activities provides maximum time for interview preparation
- A high number of interviews in a brief period of time in determined industries rapidly improves your interviewing performance
- You quickly learn the most essential information about your target companies' current status and planned future, making you an expert in the industry
- You gain confidence and momentum in your search

Peak Performance Interviewing

In traditional interviews, the candidate normally defers to the decision-maker. Don't. Even the first 10 seconds of an interview can determine who controls the tempo and discussion. You need to take immediate control of the interview in order to show how much value you will create. I call this strategy, Peak Performance Interviewing. In Peak Performance Interviewing, you make sure everything discussed at the interview is about the value you can generate for the company. It is your chance to shine.

This approach has two steps. Step one is to research the decision-maker's needs using, among other things, research meetings (see Chapter 3.2). Step two is to show the decision-maker your value proposition and value generation with a powerful Growth Agenda. Ask the decision-maker for permission to present your ideas. Your presentation shows how much you can grow the decision-maker's organization and how you will achieve this growth. Stressing your value gives you power and control.

Trigger Demand For Yourself To Overcome Organizational Inertia

Be proactive during the interviewing stage. Drive the process and overcome organizational inertia. Making quick progress in the Hidden Job Market requires a sense of urgency. Some medium-sized or large organizations are lethargic and avoid change regardless of the value you offer. For example, underperforming CEOs sometimes remain in office for years without anybody understanding why. Or it may take years before an organization fully agrees to the importance of environmental friendliness and sustainability, and even longer until it hires a Director for Corporate Social Responsibility or outsources that role to an agency.

Develop A Highly-customized, Low-risk Solution

Hidden jobs rarely go to those with preconceived, ready-made solutions, but rather to people who engineer their initial value proposition, step-by-step, conversation after conversation, into a workable, low-risk solution for the hiring organization.

As you meet more people in your target organizations, you need to dig deeper into the organizational bottlenecks through repeated questions and frequent feedback. Fine-tune your solution not only to the decision-maker but also to the surrounding leadership team. You must address each interviewer's priorities and needs. You will become a must-hire by positioning your solution proposal as closely as possible to the decision-maker's and most stakeholders' needs and selling yourself as THE solution provider to hire.

Your Hidden Job Market Advisor is an invaluable asset to help you optimize your value during this process.

5.2 THE GROWTH AGENDA

Present A Growth Agenda To Win The Job Interview

The best way to assert your value and show your performance is to present a Growth Agenda. The Growth Agenda is a document that sells you to the decision-maker. It is proof that investment in you is the best solution.

Shareholder Value

Your Growth Agenda must align with shareholder value, because your job offer relates to it. Shareholders are those who hire and fire top executives through the board. Total Shareholder Return[7] is your performance yardstick. Once you align your Growth Agenda to shareholder value you can then consider value for other stakeholders, foremost among them employees and customers.

For corporate America, shareholder goals mean revenue and profit margin. However, you should also consider the sustainability of this value. Show short-term (6 to 12 months) and long-term (3 to 5 years) growth to support sustainable shareholder value. Too much emphasis on quarterly goals can hurt long-term initiatives and sustainability. Therefore, offer maximum and sustainable shareholder value.

Benefits Of The Growth Agenda

The Growth Agenda gives you a significant edge compared with other candidates during the interview process.

Benefits include:

- Showing your preparation and commitment to this opportunity
- Proving your ability to do the job and how much profit you will generate
- Reducing the risk in your hiring
- Giving you confidence, since you stand in front of the interviewer and talk as if you were already working inside the organization
- Placing yourself in a position of power and control
- Allowing your personality and passion to shine

I cannot exaggerate the powerful impression you create by presenting an outstanding Growth Agenda. I know one chief executive officer-level job seeker who prepared and presented such a great plan that his interviewers dismissed a phone call from a past employer warning them about the candidate's temper. Ultimately, the decision-maker's hiring of this candidate based on the Growth Agenda proved to be the correct decision. This CEO candidate produced stellar results and his behavior was beyond reproach.

A Living Document As You Move Forward

Your Growth Agenda becomes better and more valuable as you proceed through interviews with the hiring organization. Regularly update and refine it. I am a firm believer in the value of preparing and presenting the Growth Agenda because it is one of the best ways to communicate the value of your ideas.

Create a concise Growth Agenda of around 8 to 20 pages covering the first 6, 12, and 18 months of your work at the decision-maker's organization. Depending on the industry, other documents or samples such as customer testimonials, list of patents, designer portfolios, etc., may also be recommended.

A Winning Start For Your Interview – How To Kick Off Your Presentation

Immediately after you exchange greetings, names and business cards, you need to ask the interviewer for permission to present your Growth Agenda. Simply state you want to share some ideas about (your topic of presentation).

Let me repeat: Immediately! Do not wait until you are seated and the interviewer begins asking standard interview questions. This is too late. He then expects you to answer his questions, not ask questions. You will have missed your chance.

The Growth Agenda allows you to take control of the interview. You are no longer reacting to the interviewer. Instead you are dictating the topic of conversation. Moreover, this action improves your chances of showing your irresistible value.

The Three Essential Parts Of An Effective Growth Agenda For Interviews

There are three essential questions the interviewer needs to know.

1. **WHO:** Who are you? What is unique about you?
2. **WHAT:** What value do you bring?
3. **HOW:** How will you execute?

The Structure Of Your Growth Agenda

Break your Growth Agenda down into three parts:

1. **The decision-maker's problem:** What is the current situation of the organization and the hiring unit's business? What problems do they have?

2. **Vision:** What are your vision and goals? What do you want to achieve in 3, 6, 12 and 18 months? What is your strategy? How do you want to achieve your goals?

3. **Specific action:** How will you implement your strategy? What specific actions will you take?

Be sure to include which of your accomplishments justify your claims. What strong proof do you have that supports your position? For example, show them testimonials from high-profile customers, solid third-party endorsements, increases in market share, annual sales turnovers, awards or articles in reputable publications.

Finally, conclude that you are the best possible choice for the decision-maker because only you can execute this Growth Agenda.

Your presentation should be between 7 to 15 minutes and concise. Bullet-point format is effective. Make it visually attractive. Bring physical objects, samples, and prototypes that help you get your ideas across effectively.

Talk Like A Peer in The Boardroom

Talk as if you already have the job. Behave as if you were already part of the leadership team. Your attitude determines your success.

Create Alignment Between Different Stakeholders

Reaching consensus is about creating alignment between different stakeholders who hold different priorities and interests. Customize Your Value Proposition and Growth Agenda to create this alignment. This way, you create specific value for each important stakeholder.

Vision, People And Strategy

Your Growth Agenda must also bringpresent your vision and your strategy for achieving this vision. You must therefore explain how you plan to lead, engage and motivate people towards this final goal.

Work With Your Hidden Job Market Advisor

The Hidden Job Market Advisor as Sparring Partner and Sounding Board

The Hidden Job Market Advisor acts as a sparring partner and sounding board to maximize your interview performance by (but not only)focusing on but not being limited to optimizing your Value Proposition and Growth Agenda.

Case Study

I received a request from an executive to help him with his CEO job search. I began coaching him using the Morita Method, and soon afterward, this Morita Executive became the new CEO of AB Corp. The following paragraphs describe how this successful engagement came about.

The Morita Method Executive

The Morita Executive was a late forties General Manager of a new division within a multinational industrial conglomerate. He was earning over USD $300,000. Although he had a successful track record, he felt dissatisfied by big company politics, slow corporate decision-making, and limited freedom to implement innovative changes in his division. He felt that the company's current path was limiting its business development and overall competitiveness. He yearned to work with a more entrepreneurially-driven, fast-growth, and medium-sized company with a great team, one eager to aggressively expand and build a global business.

AB Corp's Hidden CEO Opportunity

The board of AB Corp, a medium-sized company, decided to fire its underperforming CEO, who was an external hire and had been in office for only 12 months. His mission had been to further develop and globally commercialize a promising security software solution. The board was in the process of defining the specifications for the fired CEO's successor, but urgency was leading them to begin considering candidates before these specifications were completed. The board had some hesitation in bringing an external hire due to its poor experience with its previous external hire.

The Morita Method in Action

The Morita Method Executive and I jointly identified the opportunity to interview with AB Corp for the CEO position.

To get the executive in peak performance for his interview, I coached him on the following activities:

- Ensured consistency in the Growth Agenda in terms of core message, Unique Value Proposition, vision, goals, strategy and execution.

- Role-played different interview scenarios, including why the executive will not make the same mistakes that the previous CEO was fired for.

- Rehearsed key parts and key phrases to ensure superior delivery.

- Speaking briefly, persuasively and assertively.

- Congruence in his presentation (words, thoughts, body language, etc.).

Along with the above, I did the following to give the Morita Executive outstanding advantage.

- Identified and connected with a trusted contact of the interviewer for a research meeting.

- Researched the interviewer's background for points of leverage. For example, the interviewer had a strong background in risk management, which led to greater emphasis on risk containment in the Growth Agenda.

- Prepared tough, yet smart questions for the end of the interview.

Throughout the process, I made myself available on short notice for telephone calls to clarify critical issues the Morita Method Executive was struggling with.

The Interview

The Morita Method Executive and I prepared a Value Proposition Letter and executive resume that appealed directly to the Head of the CEO Selection Committee.

The CEO Selection Committee interviewed two candidates, the Morita Method Executive and one internal candidate, their COO. The Head of the Selection Committee described the COO as a steady performer and strong in execution. However, he didn't feel the COO was a good match for the CEO role due to his lack of charisma and entrepreneurial drive that were key requirements for their ideal candidate. Furthermore, the COO had a good vision and strategy, but didn't inspire confidence for creating new business in overseas markets. At best, the COO was an "acceptable" candidate. His interview performance was good, but far from great.

Thus, the Morita Method Executive, despite his inherent disadvantage of being an external hire, had a window of opportunity. An excellent interview that showed the desired charisma and entrepreneurship along with a Growth Agenda that explained how new overseas markets would be acquired would easily push him to the front of the pack.

Unfortunately, at first, the Morita Method Executive did not consider the needs/interests of Head of the Selection Committee and only focused on industry performance, which would not have relieved AB Corp of its reluctance to hire outside the company.

On the other hand, by working with a Hidden Job Market Advisor like myself, the Morita Method Executive prepared an impeccable interview that would only push the hiring process forward.

The result was an interview that provided a business strategy that was exactly what the Head of the Selection Committee needed to solve some of AB Corp's major problems. The Morita Method Executive described his goal to push the company away from diversification, expensive M&A and indirect sales with low profit margins to one where AB Corp evolves into a one product, one market company model. He showed how his globalization expertise would allow for AB Corp to expand its market away from its small niche and gain sufficient economies of scale and strong market leadership. He also gave numbers, explaining how he would achieve superior shareholder value by increasing profits by 30% in year 1, 54% in year 2, and 50% in year 3, and doubling both revenue and profit in 24 months.

MOST IMPORTANT: Impress the interviewer with a knockout presentation of your Growth Agenda to show you can be relied upon more than any potential competing candidate.

THE FIRST STEP: Work with your Hidden Job Market Advisor to prepare an outstanding Growth Agenda.

5.3 INTERVIEW FOLLOW-UP THAT SETS YOU APART

Wait And Lose

All career and job search experts agree on the importance of the interview follow-up. Saying "thank you" is a simple but too often forgotten courtesy.

Send A Thank You Note To The Interviewer Immediately After The Interview.

Ninety-five percent of people looking for jobs neglect this important and simple step in the job search process. A prompt interview follow-up is what can make the difference between somebody who shows commitment and everyone else.

You must send a thank you note. To emphasize just how important this note is, think of it not as a "thank you" note but rather as a "moving forward" or "getting-closer-to-offer" note. Appendix 6 shows an example of a thank you note.

In addition to saying thank you, convey one key message to the interviewer.

Depending on your case, give your thank you note an extra spin by emphasizing:

- Skill match
- Fit with team
- Unique value proposition
- Value creation
- And, if necessary, repair and recover from poor interview performance.

What matters most is that the letter is genuine and rings true. Don't exaggerate, don't understate.

When To Send

Send it on the same day as the interview or at the latest within 24 hours. Therefore, you should prepare the thank you note on letter paper before the interview, so that you can immediately dispatch your thank you message. Send one note to each interviewer. Make sure to personalize each message depending on the interaction you had.

The Format Is Up To You

Any format will do as long as the message reaches the interviewer in a timely manner. Calling, emailing, mailing or faxing are all fine. A handwritten or typed card sent in addition to a previous e-mail message is a legitimate and effective follow-up.

A speedy and persistent follow-up:

- Sets you apart from other candidates
- Shows you are committed and interested
- Keeps your name and your agenda in their mind
- Reminds the interviewer to take the next step

MOST IMPORTANT: Be among the five percent of professionals who stand out by sending a thank you note to their interviewer.

THE FIRST STEP: Customize and complete the thank you message.

5.4 FINALIZING THE OFFER

Pay For Performance

The Morita Method subscribes to Pay for Performance which enables you to explain to decision-makers at the hiring organization:

- How can you create shareholder value?
- What is fair remuneration for value-based contribution?

Pay for Performance is an important way to differentiate yourself in the Hidden Job Market. By associating your pay with **shareholder value, you will quickly come to an agreement on a compensation package you deserve.**

Tie Pay To Sustainable Value

Tie Pay for Performance to short-term (6 to 12 months) and long-term (3 to 5 years) shareholder goals to create sustainable value. For corporate America, shareholder goals mean revenue and profit margin. Your mission to finalize the offer is not only to satisfy sustainable revenue and profit margins, but also to show a sustainable strategy for your business plan execution.

Back Up Your Demands With Evidence

Create a simple Compensation Package Overview in an excel sheet, bring it to the interview, and hand it to the decision-maker should there be disagreement regarding compensation. Furthermore, be ready to supply compensation data about peer companies to back up your demands. Leave no doubt that you are reasonable.

You are more hirable when having reasonable demands. Your pay demands must be within reasonable limits of what other companies in similar or related industries are paying. PepsiCo states in their proxies: "Pay levels for executive officers are designed to be competitive relative to our peer group companies and, most importantly, align with the Company's performance. Pay-for-performance is a critical policy in designing our executive officer compensation."

Pay for Performance makes a large portion of your compensation variable. As your variable portion increases, so does the gain potential, but also the risk. It all the more urges you to do your due diligence about your hidden opportunity and not only look at the pros but especially the cons for you and your career.

MOST IMPORTANT: Pay for Performance based on shareholder value helps you to differentiate yourself in the Hidden Job Market.

THE FIRST STEP: Make clear your impact on revenue and profit margins.

5.5 ON-BOARD SUPPORT

Bridging The Transition Challenge Through Successful On-boarding

The Morita Method sets the highest standards for job search success. Success includes, however, not only signing a job offer, but also paramount performance in your new job.

The 100 Day Challenge

In today's fast-moving world, the executive really has to set his agenda in his first 100 days. This early and short period establishes your reputation at the organization. Many companies provide on-board coaching to help this transition.

Negotiate An On-board Coaching Package

Present on-board coaching as a win-win arrangement because it is of mutual interest and benefit. Your first 100 days are pivotal to you and the hiring organization. On-board coaching achieves high performance faster and assures you and the whole organization that you will achieve your goals. Your Hidden Job Market Advisor is deeply familiar with you and the target organization and can effectively help achieve maximum results through effective on-board coaching.

Most executives don't ask for professional transitional support because they underestimate the risks of external hiring. Research has shown that up to 40% of external executive hires end in failure. Too many executives endure avoidable pitfalls because they are unprepared for the company culture of decision-making and actions.

To Create Momentum, You Need To Identify And Mobilize Those Essential For Your Success

The stakes are high. Failure can cost you your job and be a serious blow to your career. The company will lose too, as its hiring an effective leader will be delayed and it risks a loss of markets, clients and workforce. This is why Human Resources Directors are recognizing the need to invest in an on-board coach who helps you track and achieve your goals faster.

Added Value Through On-board Coaching From The Hidden Job Market Advisor

Many Human Resources departments provide some form of on-board coaching. However, their internal perspective and orientation is both helpful and a hindrance. It's helpful because they know the company, they know its history, and they can provide insights about people and departments. At the same time, it often lacks an outsider's perspective. They can't provide a multi-industry perspective and often resist implementing what works well in other organizations. That's where the Hidden Job Market Advisor comes in.

What matters during negotiations is not solely agreement for on-board support, but the quality of the support. I strongly recommend you encourage the organization to welcome your Hidden Job Market Advisor who has seen you get this far.

CONCLUSION

"Why haven't you found a job yet?" Most people answer, "I cannot find any opportunities," or "There are no opportunities." The very same people are surprised to hear that there is a Hidden Job Market, where at least 80% of all job opportunities can be found. If you look at the hundreds of thousands of positions filled at a salary of $100,000 or more in the United States' Hidden Job Market alone, you know that there are plenty of opportunities.

The question "Why haven't I found a job?" is a symptom of the pain, frustration, and procrastination that many suffer from having the wrong focus and the wrong approach. From this moment forward, change your focus and approach from open to hidden jobs.

You have to market and manage yourself as a business. Executive jobs are investment projects or joint ventures for Me Inc.

With the **mindshift towards entrepreneur of your career**, you will understand that your job search is about knowing who you are and what you want from life and your career. Self-discovery will reveal what you want from life and your career. Passion will create outstanding value for you in your next job for your next company and its customers.

Find your perfect job, not just any job. Go beyond money, title, company and location. Dare to be bold and design your perfect job using the Job Temple.

EXECUTIVE JOB SEARCH IN THE HIDDEN JOB MARKET

With an entrepreneurial attitude and a vision of your next job you set out a direct mail job search campaign to chase your favorite companies. The world is your stage.

A dramatic increase in the number of executive appointments is what will get you conversations with decision-makers and ultimately several job offers. Select the one closest to your perfect job.

Learn to focus on the essential: getting interviews.

To that end, outsource to your Hidden Job Market Advisor.

The essence of the Morita Method is that it brings you the vital number of interviews needed for multiple job offers.

This is hard work, but be assured, be persistent: the taste of success is always rewarding.

TERMINOLOGY	
Unique Value Proposition	The unique value the Morita Method Executive offers to his/her target organization
Executive resume	Resume for executives
Decision-makers	The person or group ultimately responsible for hiring of an executive
6-figure executives	Executives with $150,000-unlimited compensation
Growth Agenda	Your plan on how to help the decision-maker grow his business
Peak Performance Interviewing	Achieve best interview performance by delivering maximum value for the decision-maker in interviews
Morita Method Executive	Executive who gives Hidden Job Market Advisor Rainer Morita a mandate
Hidden Job Interview	Interview surrounding a hidden job opportunity

APPENDIX 1:
OTHER JOB SEARCH CHANNELS

While I advocate direct mail, there are other job search channels that, depending on you and your target industry, may be worth considering

OTHER CHANNEL 1: COLD CALLING

What Is Cold Calling?

Cold calling is telephone calling decision-makers or their subordinates to arrange an interview.

What Matters Most: Your Unique Value Proposition

When you call, you must be ready with your unique value proposition, which will propose to the decision-maker value that he will find irresistible. Just as for direct mail, the value you offer determines the odds of you meeting.

Who Should Use Cold Calling?

For me cold calling is thrilling and exciting. What about you? Do you feel at ease calling total strangers for interviews and being rejected most of the time? If not, cold calling is not for you. Consider other job search techniques. Even if you are a quick learner and take on the challenge of cold calling, it will take at least two to four weeks to achieve results. This is a long time given you want to finish your job search in 120 days.

Cold Callings Skills

I strongly recommend buying a book on essential cold calling skills. Enjoying cold calling is not enough; you must also do it well.

The main skills you need to learn are as follows:

- Overcoming fear of rejection
- Handling objections
- Techniques for getting most of your voicemails returned
- Techniques for calling mobile phones
- Getting through screeners or gatekeepers
- Planning and measuring progress
- Learning from telephone scripts and developing your own.

Overcome Your Fear Of Rejection

Many people dislike cold calling for the same reason they dislike selling door-to-door. Too many rejections, not enough success. But that is the nature of cold calling. Be honest with yourself when deciding to invest your time and resources into cold calling.

Why Use Cold Calling?

Cold calling puts your job search on the fast track. Cold calling is an effective method for booking interviews quickly. You are in full control because it is the one method that has you directly talking to the decision-maker. Executive recruiters are heavy cold callers because it gives instantaneous results.

Demerits Of Cold Calling

Cold calling comes at a price:

- **It is expensive:** making thousands of phone calls for a limited number of interviews, especially if you are searching for a job outside your home country can be costly.
- **It is very time-consuming:** you have to speak to many people or automated machines before reaching the decision-maker.

- **You have only one chance:** if the decision-maker is busy or in a bad mood, your value will never be recognized.

Phone Scripts

Prepare scripts for your phone calls. Practice on your own and with your Hidden Job Market Advisor. Gradually, you will lose your fear of cold calling and speak with a strong and confident voice.

"Hello Mr. Smith, I'm (your name). I heard that your division *won the contract to supply your innovative fine chemical compounds to DuPont for their product X* (this is the "What's behind the story?" or the reasons why hidden jobs exist). *I worked for DuPont both as a hands-on engineer and engineering manager* (your unique sales point) and want to share with you *my strategy or you for penetrating the entire DuPont Division as well as improving your product fit for DuPont* (Unique Value Proposition). When could we meet over the next two weeks for 30 minutes in your office?"

Research For Cold Calling

For you to rely on cold calling, you need to create a target list of similar size to that of a direct mailing campaign prior to your calling. In other words, you will need thousands of leads. Find a data researcher and outsource the task of creating a calling list for you.

MOST IMPORTANT: Turn cold calling into smart calling by confidently offering the decision-maker irresistible value. The finer the bait, the shorter the wait.

THE FIRST STEP: Create your Unique Value Proposition.

OTHER CHANNEL 2: EXECUTIVE RECRUITERS

> **EXECUTIVE RECRUITERS GIVE YOU LEVERAGE, IF YOU OFFER TOP VALUE, AND IF YOU ARE ABLE TO COMMUNICATE IT.**

Although the Morita Method insists you use direct mail as a job search channel, no channel may be more effective than that of the recruiter. Excellent executive recruiters have networks in your target industry that are second to none and have non-public information that is perfect when operating in the Hidden Job Market. However, executive recruiters are a selective group, only wanting to work with top value generators. Unless you are convinced that you too are a top value generator, I would encourage you to focus on the other job search channels described in this book. Or, ask executive recruiters up front the following questions: On a scale from one to ten, how attractive is my profile for hiring organizations and my job search goals? Am I competitive enough to proceed to the final stages and be shortlisted against other competing candidates?

How Good Am I At Interviewing With Executive Recruiters?

> **AM I GOOD AT INTERVIEWING IN GENERAL AND PRESENTING MY VALUE TO EXECUTIVE RECRUITERS IN PARTICULAR?**

Executive recruiters are not your friends. They are extensions of hiring organizations. Essentially, meeting with an agent of the decision-maker or meeting with the decision-maker directly, is the same. Especially if you go the extra mile and travel a long way to meet face-to-face with the executive recruiter, you must shine and perform well in that meeting.

Mid-fifties Executives Over-rely On Executive Recruiters

If you are the high-powered in-demand executive that executive recruiters value and woo, disregard this warning. If not, my following advice will save you from frustration. Many mid-fifties executives should avoid executive recruiters. The market is against you when using this brokerage.

Who Hires Executive Recruiters

Many people assume that executive recruiters are agents who find individuals jobs. The truth is, executive recruiters are contracted Human Resources Specialists hired by a company to fill a position.

Much like how you would not expect the Human Resources department of a company to reply to you unless you had a perfect profile, do not expect a recruiter to reply to you unless you can show top value.

Companies that hire recruiters are already paying a premium for you, as along with your annual salary they pay the recruiter a fee that equals 20% to 40% of your annual salary. Therefore, the decision-maker expects to only be hiring the best candidates, which means the recruiter will only introduce the best candidates.

Clearly State Your Compensation

Your communication to executive recruiters should state clearly your total compensation, because executive agencies categorize and match-make executives according to their pay.

What An Executive Recruiter May Do For You

Some people assume that upon registering with a recruiter, you sit back and let him do all the work. Although executive recruiters are unlikely to give support similar to that of a job search coach, their occasional on-the-spot advice can be worth gold. A good partnership means that the recruiter is helping you with introductions to decision-makers, and possibly also with improvements in your Value Proposition Letter and executive resume as well as preparation for interviews.

Finally, as in any profession, the difference between a strong and poor executive recruiter will have big effects on your job search. Still, as good as a recruiter is, do not rely on him to get the bulk of your interviews. Remember that this is just one of many job search channels.

Finding And Contacting Executive Recruiters

Ironically, while I advocate direct mailing a Value Proposition Letter to decision-makers, the best way to contact executive recruiters in the United States is to send them your executive resume by e-mail. You can find executive recruiters through recruiter associations.

Furthermore, contact many and do not focus just on large global agencies. Quite often, small boutique agencies that specialize in an industry have invaluable insights and leads.

MOST IMPORTANT: Executive recruiters give you leverage because they are an extension of hiring organizations.

THE FIRST STEP: Clarify your Unique Value Proposition and decide whether your value offers enough to incentivize executive recruiters to partner with you.

OTHER CHANNEL 3: LINKEDIN

LinkedIn is the de facto business social networking site, with 260 million registered users as of 2013. Regardless of Open or Hidden Job Markets, LinkedIn is an excellent free tool for finding people with valuable information. Take the short time to make a professional page that will help you contact decision-makers.

Find Or Be Found?

LinkedIn is a tool that helps you find or be found. Many decision-makers and executive recruiters use it to find excellent candidates. But for our purpose and our short 120-day window, we shall use it to find.

How To Mine LinkedIn In The Hidden Job Market

I summarize the best assets LinkedIn offers to your job search:

1. **Finding Target Companies:** A simple search by industry yields a wealth of companies and C-level professionals. This can help you focus in on your targets when considering your mailing list.

2. **Finding people who know decision-makers:** LinkedIn search tools not only get you the names of decision-makers, they provide a list of people who know the decision-makers. These are people who will know the decision-maker"s needs and can provide insight on the values you need to articulate.

3. **This same feature can also help you contact people for research meetings,** be it either to learn more about an industry or company, or to help you prepare for your interview. Current and former employees can be readily found.

4. **The movement of people is an indirect indicator of hidden jobs.** Departing people are an excellent source of information about decision-makers or other key staff as well as for understanding

company needs. Newly hired managers are excellent targets for hidden jobs because they like to build up their own team and replace low performers with high performers.

Use LinkedIn Company Follow

LinkedIn Company Follow is a tool that enables you to follow the companies of your choice. It gives access to company news, blog posts, jobs, company twitter posts, event notifications and other company updates.

This tool is especially useful for job seekers who want to research companies, seek people they know at the target organization and track people joining or leaving your target organization.

How To Follow A Company On LinkedIn:

- Sign in to LinkedIn (you'll need to register)
- Click on Companies
- Search by Company Name, Keyword, or Location
- Click on the Company Page

Then, to follow companies you have interest in and to get the latest updates, click the star icon at the top right of the company page.

MOST IMPORTANT: For your 90-day search, mine and reach out to people identified through LinkedIn.

THE FIRST STEP: Identify people on LinkedIn for research meetings.

OTHER CHANNEL 4: PERSONAL CONTACTS

Use Your Personal Contacts To Find Hidden Job Market Opportunities

Personal contacts fall into two categories:

1. Private
2. Business

Generally, business contacts are more valuable than private ones.

Listing Your Personal Contacts

It is said that any person has at least 150 personal contacts, but few actually remember them. That is why you should create a list of your personal contacts.

Rating Your Contacts

Rate and prioritize your contacts using two criteria:

1. Their power to hire you or their proximity to those who can
2. The likelihood they will support your Unique Value Proposition and dream job search.

Ask For References, Not Jobs

In a tough economy, personal contacts of influence tend to be inundated with unsolicited job inquiries. This is especially true during restructuring waves in an industry. "Oh, no, not another one" is what your contacts think when bombarded with sudden job inquiries.

I therefore recommend you ask for references. Your personal contacts are more likely to respond favorably to this request than one for a job. Thus, you will have secured a positive reaction and therefore can engage them in deeper conversation about you, your goals and your background. The odds are then in your favor that a personal contact might introduce you to somebody needing you or pointing you to hot hidden job opportunities.

The Merits Of Personal Contacts For Your Job Search In The Hidden Job Market

Personal contacts have many attractive aspects as a job search channel.

- **Fast decision-making and hiring process:** The hiring process is much shorter, since people know you already. In some cases, a hiring may happen after only one meeting.
- **Less risk and more trust:** The decision-maker is less hesitant with you because of the established relationship.
- **Less stress:** Dealing with people you know is easier and more enjoyable.

How To Find Personal Contacts

Social media such as LinkedIn, Xing or Facebook have built-in functions to find and connect with lost acquaintances at work or college. Also try metasearch engines such as SavvySearch *(www.savvysearch.com)* or MetaCrawler *(www.metacrawler.com)* that aggregate results from different search engines.

MOST IMPORTANT: Personal contacts are worth gold. Use them wisely as a lever for your job search in the Hidden Job Market.

THE FIRST STEP: Create a list of your personal contacts.

OTHER CHANNEL 5: NETWORKING

Network With People, Not Computers

Networking is about meeting people in pursuit of your perfect job.

Job seekers mistakenly believe that networking is only for acquiring job interviews. There are, in fact, many reasons to network: research meetings, get-to-know-each-other meetings, candidate-in-waiting interviews, etc. Despite the popularity of the Internet and social media, networking is all about talking to people face-to-face. Computer-to-computer interactions are fine to establish first contacts, but you must interact with people.

> **REMEMBER, PEOPLE HIRE YOU, NOT COMPUTERS.**

Who Can Ask For Referrals?

Anyone. This is why referrals are so important.

How To Ask For Referrals

Learning how to ask for referrals effectively will turbocharge your job search. It will help you reach the people you need to talk to. The first thing to understand is that people like to help. It is part of human nature. When you ask people to support you in your job search, it resonates with them.

> **LEARN HOW TO ASK FOR REFERRALS.**

However, you need to master the art of asking for referrals in order to do it well. I repeat, you must learn how to ask people The Right Way. A lot of job seekers get few introductions because they ask in the wrong way.

Examples Of Referral Questions:

- You are looking for a general manager job in a US software company in Japan:

- Who do you know that is a worldwide sales vice president with a U.S. software company located in California?

- You are looking for a regional sales director job in a Canadian semiconductor company in China:

- Who do you know that is an Asia-Pacific general manager with a Canadian semiconductor company?

The First Steps Towards Increasing Referrals In The Hidden Job Market:

- Create your own referral questions ("Who do you know that is...?") and test them.

Do's And Don'ts When Asking For Referrals

Follow these Do's and Don'ts to maximize your number of referrals.

Do's

- **Be as accurate and precise as possible** in regard to the referrals you need. Don't reduce your chances to zero by asking for the impossible.

- **In case your personal contacts don't know anyone,** ask for introductions to people whose referrals will match your criteria.

- **Network with a giving attitude** towards the person you meet.

- **Be concise.** One question is best. One explanation followed by a question will also do.

- **Specify that you are looking for a direct introduction** or only the name, telephone number and email address of the referral.

- **Practice asking for referrals** with your Job Search Support Team.

Don'ts

- **Never wait for things to happen.** Don't ask the person you asked for a referral to only pass your contact information to the person in question. Either ask the person to arrange a meeting or ask for the third person's contact information.

- **Avoid yes/no questions like "Do you know anybody...?"** because it invites people saying, "No, I am sorry." Remember, the master way of starting referral questions is "Who do you know that is ...?"

- **Do not always accept "No."** That answer could be because of your poor question. Be sure that the person you are asking has not misunderstood your request. Politely confirm that no one in his or her network can help you.

Be Somebody – Have Your Business Card Ready

Network like a professional. Always carry your business cards with you. Especially if you are unemployed, always carry impeccable business cards that show not only your name but your brand, image and specialization instantly. This may sound old-fashioned, but how else do you want to make credible contacts with executives?

MOST IMPORTANT: Maximize your time talking face-to-face with people.

OTHER CHANNEL 6: TARGETED NETWORKING

Less Is More – Focus On The Vital Few

Networking is often local or tied to certain events. It also tends to be less focused in terms of outcome. Who exactly are you going to meet at that event is often outside of your control. The underlying assumption is that you have hopes and believe that this event or this person will lead you to the next step in your job search. This rather passive attitude and random approach is difficult to accept for the Morita Method Executive. What will you do if your favorite event takes place only once a year, far away from your home and the people you want to network with are not attending? This is where Targeted Networking comes in. It makes the rather random networking more focused because every networking action is based on specific targets.

Targeted networking is all about engaging with people who are best positioned to introduce you to decision-makers. These include people you do not even know.

According to Richard Koch, the author of the business classic about the Pareto Law, *The 80/20 Principle,* our top six business relationships account for more than all the rest of our contacts. No more than six people. He points out that 80% of the value of our relationships comes from 20% of our relationships. Are you one of those who, according to Koch, spend much too little of your attention on the 20% of relationships that creates 80% of that value?[9]

> **FOCUS ON THE VITAL FEW.**

That is why I want you to concentrate on the vital few rather than the many others.

Targeted Networking Approach

Pick the one company you most want to join. From there, identify decision-makers and then *connectors,* those who can introduce you to these decision-makers. Connectors can be people you know (personal contacts) or not know (networking contacts). LinkedIn or Xing are useful tools for this purpose.

Your Springboard: Making Vital Connections

Reach out to people of the highest ranks in society and organizations. Company executives, tycoons, celebrities, thought leaders, politicians, and aristocrats are among the type of people that could make powerful introductions and open doors to many hidden jobs.

Your dream job is often as difficult to realize as you want it to be and not as it really is. Contact people you consider impossible to reach.

How I Met The Ex-President Of Toyota Motor Corporation

One of the industries I specialize in as a Hidden Job Market Advisor is the automotive industry. Hiroshi Okuda is one of the biggest names in this industry and is the previous President of Toyota Motor Corporation, where he still acts as an advisor. He was also President of Keidanren, the most powerful Japan Business Federation.

Most normal people would consider it impossible to make contact with him. So how did I meet him?

I registered for an event organized by the American Chamber of Commerce in Japan where Okuda was invited as a speaker. After his presentation, I sought him out and exchanged business cards with him.

In the same way, I met with the president of Mazda Corporation and the vice president of R&D of Daimler AG, just to name a few.

The lesson for you is that you can meet anyone in the world at events, be it the International Consumer Electronics Show in Las Vegas, the Davos World Economic Forum, the Economist Conferences or the Foreign Correspondents Club Events in Tokyo. Choose an event, go there and meet the person of your choice.

Find Connectors In Groups The Decision-maker Belongs To

Connectors are sometimes affiliated with networking groups or associations such as Chambers of Commerce and Industry, charities, exclusive membership clubs such as Lions Club or Rotary Club, alumni groups (college, high school), sports and fitness clubs and so on. Use LinkedIn or other social media to find groups your target executive belongs. Then identify and approach those individuals that share the same group or association with your target executive and, finally, ask these people for an introduction.

How To Use Your Connector After An Event Meeting

Your ultimate goal is to meet decision-makers. During your first encounter with a connector you exchange business cards. The next step is to follow up and make an appointment with the person. Remember, your goal is to meet the decision-maker. Sometimes it is best to bluntly ask for the introduction. Other times it is better to arrange an appointment with the connector and brief him or her on your desire to meet the decision-maker.

Meeting "To be continued…" Is Your Goal

Unless the decision-maker you are meeting has an open job, the maximum expectation you should have about your meeting outcome is a conversation to be continued. Don't jump the gun. Bite your tongue and do not ask for a job. Impatience may lead to a straightforward "No."

If you are patient, listen more than talk in order to prepare your value proposition to solve his problems. If the timing is right for the executive and the organization, you may be invited to show your solution proposal to the next level inside the organization.

The Advantages Of Targeted Networking:

- Increases the chances of discovering a hidden job when communicating directly with hiring executives.

- Increases the chances that your contact will refer a hidden job to you.

What Are The Drawbacks Of Target Networking?

Targeted networking requires communicating with strangers. This is not for everyone. Furthermore, networking one by one is time consuming. For geographically dispersed industries, networking in person can easily become unfeasible. Even attending tradeshows and exhibitions is time consuming.

Targeted networking covers only a small piece of the entire target market.

Targeted networking is ineffective and slow when aiming to cover the entire market and gain access to all hidden jobs in 120 days.

MOST IMPORTANT: Select your key relationships carefully and then build with commitment.

THE FIRST STEP: Find your top three to five business contacts for networking.

APPENDIX 2:
SAMPLE VALUE PROPOSITION LETTER

SAMPLE CHINA CEO VALUE PROPOSITION LETTER

Andrew Smith
1426 Charleston Road
Santa Monica, Los Angeles, CA, 90401, USA

Date

Mr. Decision-maker
President
Name of your Target Company
Address

Dear Mr. Decision-maker,

Would you like help with expanding your company into China and newly emerging Asian markets?

I am a series-CEO for Hong Kong subsidiaries of US machinery and machine tool manufacturers over the last 15 years, with responsibility for Hong Kong, Taiwan and China markets.

A few of my highlights include:

- Captured 25% of worldwide revenue from the Greater China markets in only four years.
- Built up executive connections with all major automotive and electronics manufacturers in Greater China.
- Achieved the highest net-revenue per head over a 10 year span for my current company while keeping employee turnover to a minimum.

I would like to explore how I can give your company a stronger presence in the Asia-Pacific Region.

Sincerely,
Andrew Smith

PS: For your information, my total compensation in recent years has been north of $500K.

SAMPLE EMERGING MARKETS CEO, INDIA VALUE PROPOSITION LETTER

Peter Jones
5, Jamshedji Tata Road,
Churchgate, Mumbai,
Maharashtra 400020, India

Mr. Decision-maker
President
Company name,
Global Headquarter Address
Date

Dear Mr. Decision-maker,

Would you like help with expanding your mobile data services into India and gain 50% market share in 12 to 18 months? Imagine an experienced Emerging Market CEO who has done it and will do it for you.

This is where I come in:

- I helped my company ABC India achieve 55% of total revenue within 18 months and made it the most data centric mobile operator in India.
- I shine where you struggle. I am well-connected with top government officials and know how to play the game with telecom authorities to promote your brand.
- In Malaysia, Indonesia and Singapore I secured early-mover advantages and a dominant market position for my company in less than 15 months.

Be the first to capture market share and early leadership in this booming market. With me at the top, you will be number one.

Let's discuss how together we can propel your brand to the next level in India.

Sincerely,
Peter Jones

PS: For your information, my total compensation in recent years has been between $250k-$300K.

APPENDIX 3:
LIST OF QUESTIONS FOR RESEARCH MEETINGS

List of questions for research meetings regarding your mailing list, value proposition, and job search goals:

- What advice do you have on improving my perfect job definition?

- What advice do you have on improving my list of target companies?

- What advice do you have on improving my Value Proposition to companies involved in my target industry?

- What advice do you have on improving my Value Proposition Letter?

- What advice do you have on improving my Job Search Goals (title, industry, compensation, location)?

List of questions relating to your target job for a research meeting:

- How did you find this job?
- What do you like most about this job?
- What do you dislike most about this job?
- What is the key performance indicator for this job?
- What skills do you need to be a top performer in this job?
- What are the main tasks of this job?
- What are the challenges you are facing as a top performer in your division?
- Please describe how people with passion for this job work differently from impassionate people?
- What skills are desirable to have, but not absolutely necessary?
- Is working from home possible for this kind of job?

- Somebody told me that success in this job requires xyz. Do you agree? Would you add something?

- What are the biggest challenges for decision-makers to grow revenue in this tough/booming economy?

- What are the priorities of top management for developing new income streams?

- What are the qualities of the best hires in your company?

- How can I demonstrate that I fit this job?

- What kinds of people do not fit this job?

- What are the salary levels for this type of job?

- What has the biggest impact on salary for this job?

- Over the last five years, have salaries been rising or falling for this type of job?

- Who do you know did not fulfill the standard requirements for this job and still got it? How?

- Who do you think is able to suggest similar careers for me based on my skills and background?

- How does maternity affect your career in this job?

- How does your company handle maternity and those mothers wishing to return to work after maternity leave is over?

- How much travel does this job require?

List of questions relating to your target industry for a research meeting:

- How did you find this industry?

- What do you like most about this industry?

- What are the challenges you are facing as a top performer in your industry?

- Who else do you know is an expert in your industry?

- Who else do you recommend to learn more about this industry?

- Which articles, newspapers, journals, books or motion pictures do you recommend to learn more about the industry?

- What are the salary levels in this industry?

- Over the last five years, have salaries been rising or falling in this industry?

- What kind of people fit/do not fit this industry?

- Which segments in this industry are growing fastest? Which one has the best prospects long-term?

- What possible threats are there for this industry?

- Which are the top three companies in this industry?

- What are the biggest trends in this industry with the potential to change the rules of the game?

- What is the average revenue growth rate of the most successful companies in this industry?

Never forget to ask for referrals before the end of the interview:

- Whom do you know in this company/industry who could help me better understand new business development issues?

- Who else do you know is an expert in this company/industry?

- Who do you know is well connected in this industry?

- Who do you recommend to learn more about this company/industry?

- Who are the people you recommend contacting in those companies/industries?

Followed by:

- Can I mention your name to people if asked?

APPENDIX 4:
SAMPLE THANK-YOU LETTER

Anthony Hogan
630-665-2986 | anthonyhogan@me.com
6150 Roosevelt Plaza, Suite 405 | Chicago, IL 60189

August 10, 2015

Dr. Ronald Smith
Detroit Wireless Control Systems Ltd.
40 Kennedy Road
Detroit, MI 48203

Re: General Manager, Aircraft & Aerospace Controls Division

Dear Dr. Smith:

Thank you for speaking with me during the Aerospace Exhibition at the Dallas Convention Center yesterday. I realize your schedule is very demanding, and I am grateful for the time you spent sharing your vision for the future of Detroit Wireless Control Systems.

As we discussed, I believe there is tremendous potential for your business in the aircraft and aerospace industry.

As General Manager of a new Aircraft and Aerospace Controls Division, I anticipate:

- Opening four major accounts within the first year: NASA, Honda Jet America, Boeing, and EMBRAER America
- Generating $50 million in annual revenue the next four years
- Delivering net profit of $10 million per year to the bottom line

My existing relationships in the aircraft and aerospace industry would allow me to penetrate key accounts and generate immediate returns. Creating this new division would enable your company to focus on the unique needs of these customers.

I would welcome the opportunity to meet with you and review my business growth plan in more detail. I am truly excited about this opportunity and am confident that I can lead Detroit Wireless Control Systems into the aircraft and aerospace controls market.

I will call your office next week. In the meantime, I can be reached at 630-665-2986 or anthonyhogan@me.com.

Sincerely,
Anthony Hogan

ENDNOTES

1. Grove, Andy as cited in "The 80/20 Principle," Koch, Robert, Nicholas Brealey Publishing, 1999. Print.

2. "Deloitte Survey: Worker Passion is Key to True Economic Recovery," Deloitte. PR Newswire, Web. 4 November 2010.

3. Iacocca, Lee as cited in "IACOCCA – Lee Iacocca with William Novak," Endnotes Publishing, Business News (2013-02-15). (Kindle Locations 116-120). Kindle Edition.

4. Frost, Robert, "Two Tramps In Mud Time," in *A Further Range,* New York: Henry Holt and Company, 1936. Print.

5. Blankfein, Lloyd. "Commencement Address." LaGuardia Community College. New York. 2013.

6. *Total Shareholder Return* is a measure of the performance of the company's stocks and shares over time. It is expressed as an annualized percentage of the share price appreciation and dividends paid to shareholders.

7. Onassis, Aristotle as cited in "Twist of Faith: The Story of Anne Beiler, Founder of Auntie Anne's Pretzels," Beiler, Anne, Thomas Nelson Inc, 2010. Print.

8. Hatch, Denison and Jackson, Don. "2,239 Tested Secrets For Direct Marketing Success." McGraw-Hill Education, 1999. Print.

9. Koch, Robert, "The 80/20 Principle," Nicholas Brealey Publishing, 1999. Print.

www.MoritaMethod.com

Made in the USA
Las Vegas, NV
06 August 2022